Acedia and the Transformation of Spiritual Malaise: Essays in Honour of Martin McAlinden

First published 2019
by University of Chester Press
University of Chester
Parkgate Road
Chester CH1 4BJ

Printed and bound in the UK by the
LIS Print Unit
University of Chester
Cover designed by the
LIS Graphics Team
University of Chester

A catalogue record for this book is available
from the British Library

ISBN 978-1-908258-02-1

Acedia and the Transformation of Spiritual Malaise: Essays in Honour of Martin McAlinden

Edited by
Wayne Morris

University of Chester Press

Dedicated to
Revd Dr Martin McAlinden
(1965–2016)

Priest in the Diocese of Dromore
Director of Pastoral Theology,
St Patrick's College Maynooth

CONTENTS

vii

LIST OF FIGURES

ACKNOWLEDGEMENTS

I would like to express my profound gratitude to Revd Dr Martin McAlinden in whose honour this book has been published. I knew Martin for five years during his time studying for the Doctorate in Professional Studies at the University of Chester. I became Martin's principal supervisor for his research and he was a dream student – intelligent, thoughtful, hard-working, and creative. He was also a genuinely very nice person and it was always a pleasure to be in his company. His research had such potential and I am honoured that he thought I might be the person who could bring his ideas and research to fruition. It has been a sincere privilege to work on this book and it is offered to the Church in his name.

The process of putting this book together began with a conference held in Martin's honour at Drumalis Retreat and Conference Centre in Larne – a place very dear to Martin. I would like to thank Drumalis Retreat and Conference Centre for their generosity and hospitality as hosts for this event in June 2017. In particular, Maura Burns put a great deal of effort into collaborating with me to ensure there was an appropriate opportunity to give thanks for Martin and, on this particular occasion, to note the work he did as a theological educator at Drumalis.

At the Conference, the University of Chester conferred on Martin an Honorary Doctorate in Professional Studies – the first ever to be awarded by the University. I am extremely grateful to the Vice-Chancellor, Professor Tim Wheeler, for seeing so clearly the good reasons for making such an award, and for ensuring that the University would honour Martin in such a fitting manner. Professor Wheeler has also been supportive of seeing this book come to fruition and my gratitude is owed to him and to Dr Sarah Griffiths of the University of Chester Press without whom this book would not have been published.

Acknowledgements

During Martin's doctoral journey, he was accompanied by fellow students, members of the academic team at Chester who run the Professional Doctorate, and by colleagues from St Patrick's College, Maynooth. I am delighted that this volume includes contributions from a number of those students, as well as John-Paul Sheridan from St Patrick's College, and Elaine Graham and Dawn Llewellyn from the University of Chester. I am also thrilled that Baroness Nuala O'Loan, a very close friend of Martin, agreed to write a Foreword to this volume. Their willingness to contribute is testimony to Martin as a person and the quality and importance of the research he was pursuing for the academy, the Catholic Church in Ireland, and Christian ministry in a range of denominations.

Finally, and most importantly, this book has been put together with the kind permission and support of Martin's family. In the midst of their profound grief, they exhibited the most extraordinary generosity in allowing me – someone they did not know – to advance and write up the research Martin had begun. I hope that, for them, this book is a fitting tribute to the wonderful person they have lost, whom they loved so much and who he also loved.

Wayne Morris
Feast Day St John Vianney
Patron Saint of Parish Priests
4 August 2018

LIST OF CONTRIBUTORS

Revd Dr Martin McAlinden was a priest of the Diocese of Dromore and formerly Director of Pastoral Theology at the Pontifical University of St Patrick's College, Maynooth. He was also pursuing a Professional Doctorate in Practical Theology (DProf) at the University of Chester on the theme of 'Acedia and the Transformation of Spiritual Malaise'. He published an article on his research in the journal, *Practical Theology*, (7.4, 2015). The *Practical Theology* article was republished in 2017 as a part of the journal's '10th Anniversary Article Collection' in which ten of the best articles were selected to celebrate the anniversary of the journal and to 'showcase the growth and development' of the discipline of Practical Theology over the previous ten years.

Revd Stephen Adams is currently Rector of Cowbridge in the Diocese of Llandaff in the Church in Wales. He is a student on the Doctorate in Professional Studies in Practical Theology and is working on a thesis focussed on Collaborative Ministry in the Church in Wales.

Revd Susie Collingridge currently serves in a benefice of East Hampshire parishes in the Anglican Diocese of Portsmouth and conducts doctoral research through the University of Chester on Clergy Married to Clergy in the Church of England.

Revd Ruth Craig is a Methodist Minister stationed in Ballynahinch Methodist Church, Northern Ireland. She is also a doctoral student at the University of Chester. Her research topic is Pastoral Supervision for Clergy.

Revd Claire Dawson is an Anglican priest, was ordained in 2004, and is currently Vicar of St Mary's Church, Bramall Lane and Priest in Charge of St Augustine's Church in the Anglican Diocese of Sheffield. She is a doctoral student at the University of Chester and her thesis focusses on Working Class Women's Voices Defining a New Praxis for Urban Church.

Canon Professor Elaine Graham is Grosvenor Research Professor of Practical Theology and Director of the Doctorate in Professional Studies at the University of Chester. She is also Canon Theologian at Chester Cathedral.

Revd Gill Henwood is Parish Priest of Grasmere and Rydal in Carlisle Diocese in the Church of England and a doctoral student at the University of Chester. Her thesis focusses on the theme of Equal Marriage.

Dr Dawn Llewellyn is Senior Lecturer in Religion and Gender at the University of Chester and part of the team that runs the Doctorate in Professional Studies in Practical Theology.

Professor Wayne Morris is Professor of Contextual Theology and Director of the School of Humanities at the University of Chester. He was Martin's supervisor for his Doctorate in Professional Studies in Practical Theology.

Baroness Nuala O'Loan, DBE, MRIA is a member of the House of Lords. She is the former Police Ombudsman of Northern Ireland (1999–2007) and, since 2010, has served as Chair of the Governing Authority of the National University of Ireland, Maynooth.

Revd Dr John-Paul Sheridan is a priest of the Diocese of Ferns, Ireland. He is Education Programmes Coordinator and Lecturer at the Pontifical University of St Patrick's College, Maynooth. His postgraduate studies were undertaken at Boston College (MEd), Maynooth College (STL) and Trinity College, Dublin (PhD).

FOREWORD

Baroness Nuala O'Loan DBE, MRIA

Father Martin McAlinden was a man of huge energy – always thinking, running (in his parish they called him 'the running priest'), always looking for new thoughts, new ideas, new ways. When he began to talk to me of acedia, I did not know what he was talking about. Gradually, understanding dawned. As you read the first chapter, you will see the many attempts to define this ancient concept. Ancient it may be, yet it is truly relevant to the world today, not just for clergy and religious, but for all of us. That sense that all is not well, that in the busyness of our lives we are losing touch with the core of ourselves, that what is most precious to us is receding, disappearing in a desert of 'burnout', exhaustion, lostness, can come to all of us at different times in our lives. The consequences can be many – a drift to indifference, to triviality, to alcohol or drugs, or even to despair, as we struggle to understand what is happening. It can be a time of the utmost difficulty, when we seek answers where answers seem not be.

Gerard Manley Hopkins wrote of this thus,

> My own heart let me more have pity on; let
> Me live to my sad self hereafter kind,
> Charitable; not live this tormented mind
> With this tormented mind tormenting yet.
> I cast for comfort I can no more get
> By groping round my comfortless, than blind
> Eyes in their dark can day or thirst can find
> Thirst's all-in-all in all a world of wet.

In his moments of darkness, in the company of the Benedictines at Worth Abbey, Martin realized what had happened to him, and was graced with an understanding of how to respond in the darkness. When he had worked that out, he knew that this was something which he needed to know more about, which he needed to proclaim, to make known to so many of his priest colleagues and to others. If we can recognize the problem, we can begin to address it, and the answer Martin found was an answer which all Christians know, but few understand. It was that each of us is most fulfilled and live most in the light, when we are united to God in prayer. For it is true that busyness working for the people of God, which we interpret as being the answer to the call to holiness, can become in fact the looming cause of the loss of all that we hold dearest, all that motivates and energizes us as we seek to follow the path to holiness. It is a paradox, and in the darkness it can be almost incomprehensible: that in attempting to live our lives as the Gospel calls us to, we can lose sight of the Lord who made us all and who gave us those same Gospels.

So Martin set to work, that he might be able to explain it others. He hoped to the very end of his life that he would be able to finish the work, to share with others what he had come to understand. As illness intervened, he struggled, indeed at times in the hospice, it seemed to me he grieved that he would be unable to finish the work, though he endeavoured mightily, through chemotherapy and pain, to complete what he had set out to do. He took great consolation from the knowledge that Professor Morris, his tutor at the University of Chester, would do what he could to ensure the publication of the book, not just because he wanted publication, but because he knew that this was something which mattered, and which might help others who found themselves on similar dark journeys and who might come to realize how important it is, if we are really to come to holiness, that we make time and the space for the Lord of the work, as well as the work of the Lord. In the event he died of his cancer before he was able to bring the work forward as he had wished to do.

So it is a delight, tinged with great sadness at loss of a good friend, to see this work of love, the product of Martin's study, and of the generosity of his friends in the University of Chester, published. There is a profound message here for all who live life to the full, and are tempted to just keep going at full pace, until the darkness descends on them and they wonder what has happened. Perhaps, as a consequence of Martin's lived experience of acedia, and the analysis in this book, others may realize that they need to ensure that they, as Hopkins said,

> leave comfort root-room; let joy size
> At God knows when to God knows what; whose smile
> 's not wrung, see you; unforeseen times rather – as skies
> Betweenpie mountains – lights a lovely mile.

For there is joy and consolation in this book for those who seek it, even in desolation.

INTRODUCTION

Wayne Morris

Revd Dr Martin McAlinden was a priest of the Diocese of Dromore in Northern Ireland and, latterly, Director of Pastoral Theology at St Patrick's College, Maynooth. Martin served as a priest for twenty-six years and was much loved by his brother clergy, lay people and religious across both the North and Republic of Ireland. Having lived through his own personal struggles with his ministry, he stumbled across the ancient notion of acedia while on sabbatical at Worth Abbey. In his paper, that is the main focus of this volume, he talks about this experience in more detail. This ancient tradition of acedia spoke powerfully to his own experience of spiritual malaise. It was the 'command to pray' that helped him to hope for the possibility of moving beyond acedia to a place of renewed spiritual vitality. It was the way that acedia resonated with his own experience that led him to explore the ways in which acedia might be a useful hermeneutical lens through which to understand the experiences of crisis and struggle among Catholic priests in Ireland today. He also discovered in the ancient practices of addressing acedia a way of thinking about how priestly ministries and spiritualities today might be renewed and transformed. This led Martin to explore this more deeply through a Doctorate of Professional Studies in Practical Theology at the University of Chester.

Having completed five years of research, in June 2016, Martin died after a long struggle with cancer. During his illness, one of his primary concerns had been that the research he had done would not be wasted, but that it would be published and disseminated with a view to making a positive difference to the lives and well-being of priests in Ireland. As his doctoral supervisor, on many occasions during his illness, I encouraged him to stop and suspend his studies so that he could focus on his health, but he was very insistent that he would not

1

do that. Indeed, it became clear that his commitment to the research he had begun never waned and became one of the things that sustained, perhaps even gave him hope through his illness, and it was a profound privilege to be a part of that.

As it became clear that he was not going to finish the thesis, we had a discussion in which I promised him that if he gave the work he had so far done to me, I would do what I could to ensure that the research could be disseminated. His reason for wanting this was clear and it was his first motivation in doing his research. That reason was his love for and commitment to his brother priests in Ireland. He wanted to write something that would explore ways in which the morale and well-being of clergy had been affected in recent years by a range of factors, and Martin had been among those affected. He did not simply want to identify the problems, however, but to offer something that might be a wellspring of hope for his brother priests; a way forward that could support ministry and sustain their humanity in the future. When it was clear that Martin would not be able to complete this task himself, he asked me, as his supervisor, to do it for him. This book is the result of the promise made to him that his work would in some way be published and made available to as wide an audience as possible. I am very grateful to colleagues in the University of Chester Press for making that happen.

Taking on someone else's research is not an easy task and my ability to do justice to Martin's work is limited in many ways. As his supervisor, I was really more of a critical friend helping him to think through and push his ideas, while he was really the expert in his own subject of acedia. I am also a lay person and an Anglican so the depth of experience and personal insight that Martin brought to the research is something I could not with the best will in the world bring. So while the paper published here on acedia would have been so much better a paper had Martin completed it himself, as a poor substitute I have tried to share some of the work Martin did and to take it forward tentatively in new ways that he may have done had he been able to do so.

Introduction

The paper is published under Martin's name because, after all, this was his project and his work and it has been published with the kind and generous permission of his family. At the beginning of this process, I went through all of Martin's notes and everything he had written on acedia in order to get to grips with the research agenda he was pursuing and to understand the perspectives on this project that he was formulating. The first three chapters of the paper that follows are nearly all Martin's own words reworked into an order that would help to explain to the reader what acedia is and how he went about doing his research on this subject. Martin often wrote in the first person, using 'I' to talk about his own experience and his own views on matters. This is a paper written under his name, using his autoethnography, and so it seemed appropriate to retain his voice in this way in the work.

Martin also completed eight interviews with fellow priests in Ireland and reflections on these form the final three chapters of the paper. Had he been able to, his next task would have been to develop the themes he had begun to identify from the interviews that would speak of both experiences of and remedies for acedia in the lives of Irish Catholic priests. While much of what has been written in these final chapters has been drafted by me, the themes identified were already located within Martin's notes and so, in focussing on them, I have tried to develop themes that I suggest he would have intended to develop himself. The astute reader may notice that these chapters continue to use the first person singular from time to time, though much more sparingly than in previous chapters. Where this appears, that is also Martin's own words and voice in the paper. It is important to acknowledge that I have not, obviously, been able to check with Martin if he would be happy with what has been said in these chapters or in the paper as a whole, but I hope that he would be satisfied with the final three chapters and recognize his thoughts and voice in the words that have been written, even if it is not exactly as he would have done it.

Another complex aspect of my taking on this project is that while Martin had conducted eight interviews, transcribed them and anonymized them, the interviews were left to me to work with and use to develop the themes. The data contained in these interviews was very personal and very sensitive. The audio recordings were destroyed and I never heard them so all that I had to develop the final three chapters were the written transcripts with all the limitations of only being able to work with a fixed text rather than a living voice. Because I had no voice recordings and the transcripts had been anonymized, I have never known the identity of any of the participants who Martin interviewed.

Those who were interviewed do not know me and I do not know them either, but even without any personal connection to the people behind what I read, other than the interviewer, Martin, it was a profound privilege and honour to read those transcripts and I was deeply moved by the honesty and openness with which his interviewees shared their experiences with Martin. They were a real testament to their character and courage, as well as to the extraordinary trust they placed in their beloved friend and colleague.

I read those transcripts and they informed completely what has been written in chapters four, five and six, but because those participants have not given consent for me, rather than Martin, to use their stories, I have not included any direct quotations from the interviews. In some ways that diminishes considerably what I have been able to write, but again I was trying to hold together a difficult tension, that of fulfilling Martin's request while protecting and respecting the right to anonymity (or as Dawn Llewellyn better describes it, 'privacy') of those who generously gave their stories to Martin. I would like to assure Martin's participants that this data is safe in my care. I was given these stories because Martin trusted me and I will keep that trust.

On 16 June 2017, just a year and a day after his funeral, we held a conference at Drumalis Retreat House in Larne in honour of Martin's life and work. The University of Chester also generously conferred a much deserved posthumous honorary doctorate on Father McAlinden in recognition of his work on ecumenism, adult theological education, and practical theology and acedia in Ireland. At that conference, I presented a shorter version of the paper that follows here. For me, it was a test case. Did what I had put together from Martin's writing and notes resonate with Irish priests' experiences? Another important part of Martin's work was also his love of working with lay people in adult theological education. What was clear in his own writing was that the future of the Catholic Church in Ireland was dependent on a more confident laity, theologically resourced, who would have a crucial role to play in ensuring the well-being of the whole Church. The response to the paper given at Larne by both lay and ordained was both positive and encouraging and led me to develop and extend that initial offering into the paper contained here.

In addition, a number of students from the University of Chester, together with my colleague Dr Dawn Llewellyn, offered papers reflecting on Martin's work. The second half of this volume includes those papers and also some additional responses to the main paper and focus of this volume on acedia. The group of students who accompanied Martin on his doctoral journey were hugely influential in sustaining him intellectually, developing his thinking and motivating him to carry on, just as he was to them. Together with those of Dr Llewellyn and Revd Dr John-Paul Sheridan of St Patrick's College Maynooth, the reflections that follow Martin's paper reflect something of the ways in which his research connected with other fields of study and how the significance of what he was doing on priesthood in Ireland resonates with the challenges of priests and laity in other parts of the Catholic Church and other Christian denominations too. The volume then concludes with the text of a homily given at the Graduation Ceremony in Larne by my colleague Professor Elaine Graham.

It was a profound privilege to work with Martin and those who knew him were impacted by his character, his love for God, for other people, and his love for life itself. This book is offered in his honour as a way of ensuring a continuing legacy for the work he had begun on acedia, and to allow what he had to say about the lives of his brother priests and the renewal of the Catholic Church in Ireland to be heard.

ACEDIA AND THE TRANSFORMATION OF SPIRITUAL MALAISE

Martin McAlinden

1. INTRODUCING ACEDIA AND ME

Introduction

Beginning with describing my own encounter with acedia, this chapter attempts to introduce and understand the origins of the condition and to relate it to the main concern of this paper as a whole; that is, how acedia affects the lives of Irish Catholic diocesan clergy, and in particular to what degree it might be a catalyst for understanding and transforming the spiritual malaise these men experience. What I aim to do here is to begin to map out some of the ways that acedia provides an important hermeneutical lens through which to understand the experience of Catholic diocesan clergy in Ireland.

My Encounter with Acedia

My own introduction to acedia – to the experience and the word – was precipitated by an experience of crisis in my ministry in 2007. Despite regular pastoral supervision, my work was consuming me. I was too busy. Self-care and time off were not priorities. It felt like my vocation and belief in God were beginning to erode. At the time I described this experience as *burnout*. I negotiated a sabbatical with my bishop and used the time mainly to address my spiritual malaise. I spent a month at Worth Abbey, a Benedictine monastery in Sussex. As it happened, these four weeks coincided with Lent: spiritually I felt like I was in a wilderness. At Worth, the abbot diagnosed not burnout or any other spiritual malaise, but rather *acedia,* a word he simply described as 'spiritual sloth'. Initially I could not identify with sloth, but as I reflected it became clear that the busyness of my life as a pastor had led to a loss of taste for prayer. This in turn led to an increasingly serious cascading of symptoms: a neglect of my spiritual life and self-care, little reflective practice, a life that was becoming unmanageable and meaningless, a questioning of my vocation.

The treatment prescribed at Worth was simple; I needed to spend the month praying, and to develop a discipline of prayer when

I went home. Looking back, I can identify with DeYoung's words: 'Seeing ourselves clearly is often difficult. Sometimes we need to hear a precise diagnosis from someone else, and to hear it at a particular time' (DeYoung, 2009, 19). I intuitively knew at the time that acedia was my problem. While I went to the monastery looking for answers, amazingly, the simple command to pray was the answer I needed. So I prayed the office with the monks, listened to the story of the Exodus recited every morning, attended Eucharist, said the rosary, gave thanks for the beauty of creation as I walked in the South Downs, journalled, read spiritual books, wrote haiku poetry,[1] and spent much time in silence. In all this a transformation began to occur. I began to feel nourished again by prayer. It was this experience that led me to explore further more precisely what acedia was and the kinds of spiritual practices that could be developed to help address it.

Exploring Early Traditions of Acedia

Acedia has its roots in the deadly thought/sin tradition which came to birth in the theological reflection of the early eremitic monks[2] who lived in the fourth and fifth centuries in the deserts of Egypt, Syria and Palestine. Evagrius of Pontus was the first to write extensively about the condition, describing it as one of the eight thoughts or temptations facing monks living a life of desert solitude. While acedia attracted a lot of interest in monastic and medieval spirituality, it is surprisingly absent in many contemporary works about ministerial spirituality. In the last decade there has been an upsurge of interest in the deadly sin tradition with the temptations seen as both spiritual and psycho-spiritual conditions. Works by popular spiritual writers such as Jamison (2008) and Norris (2008) have helped revive an interest in acedia, but it continues to be an elusive term which escapes easy definition.

---

1   A traditional form of Japanese poetry.
2   An eremite is a person who lives a solitary, hermitical religious life, whereas a coenobite is a member of a monastic community.

Evagrius described acedia as the 'noonday demon' (Psalm 91:6). His context was an eremitic lifestyle in a hot, stark climate where the monk measured time by the movement of the sun. At midday, the hottest time of the day, it seemed as though the sun had stopped moving in the sky. The monk became restless and bored, perhaps lonely, and these feelings became focussed on his spiritual life. The midday sun was therefore an external stimulus, and a metaphor, which awakened the temptation to acedia. Disillusionment about the monastic life would creep in; firstly the monk noticed the lack of charity and encouragement from his brothers, and then he began to question his vocation, or as Evagrius calls it, 'the toil of the ascetic struggle'. The temptation could be to visit the sick, not out of pastoral concern but as a distraction from staying in one's cell (Evagrius, 2003, 84). The monk began to hate his cell, felt alienated from the social order of the monastery and hence the monastic life and its journey to spiritual union with God, and believed that God can be adored elsewhere. Evagrius therefore notes that this demon is the greatest obstacle to an authentic spiritual life because it can lead to a rejection of one's vocation. Unlike other passions, 'the noonday demon ... is accustomed to embrace the entire soul and oppress the spirit' (Evagrius, 1972, 26).

The Elusive Nature of Acedia

Crislip notes, Evagrius is 'neither consistent nor precise in his description of acedia' (Crislip, 2005, 145). His lengthy imagery may signify the problem (which has existed since) of clearly defining or capturing the essence of this *logismos* (*thought*) in a phrase or short sentence. This is understandable, because while the Greek word ἀκηδια (*acedia, accedie, akēdia*) has a long history in Greek literature, its precise meaning is ambiguous. Vogel recognizes that the Greek consists of an alpha-privative prefixed to the stem for 'care' or 'concern' (*kedos*), so that the most literal translation is 'carelessness' or 'lack of concern', although he acknowledges that it is extremely difficult to translate into English (Vogel, 2009, 53). Another lexicon defines ἀκηδια as 'indifference, apathy' (Amdt and Gingrich, 1979, 30). The word occurs nine times in the Septuagint where it means faintness, weariness, anguish (Wenzel, 1967, 6). In Psalm 118:28 the Revised Standard Version (RSV) translates it as 'sorrow' (*The Catholic Youth Bible Revised*, 2005, 664). Harmless and Fitzgerald, referring to Evagrius, conclude '*akēdia* is a sort of restless boredom, a listlessness, and beneath that, discouragement' (Harmless, and Fitzgerald, 2001, 510), while Wenzel characterizes Evagrius' acedia as 'psychic exhaustion and listlessness' (Wenzel, 1967, 5). To add complexity, and a consequent plethora of symptoms, Evagrius and subsequent writers relate acedia with the *logismos* of sadness. Sadness is associated with the frustration of desire and consequently may be linked to anger and is a natural reaction to loss (Tilby, 2009, 105) so symptoms approximating to depression can occur. Sadness, for the monk, can also result from 'indulging in an idealized view of past life [which undermines] the original decision to live differently' (Tilby, 2009, 112).

On an emotional scale, there is a difference between carelessness and psychic exhaustion! At this point, perhaps what is important, however, is not a precise definition of acedia emerging from Evagrius' writing, but a realisation that this temptation is fundamentally about losing one's taste for the spiritual life, is manifested in carelessness about disciplines that nurture the spiritual life, and presents as a variety of somatic and psychological symptoms which Crislip suggests are 'mutually contingent and dialectically impinging upon each other' (Crislip, 2005, 146).

Acedia and My Vocation

The experience of these monks, as Evagrius explained it, resonated deeply with my own ongoing struggles with my vocation and spiritual life. It was as if the busyness of ministry had taken me away from my true self, from my core identity, from my reason for being a priest. It was at Worth that I began to find myself again in my relationship with God, began to believe at a deep level that it is in Christ I live and move and have my being (Acts 17:28). A number of synchronicities occurred, not least my presence at the monastery during Lent, with its overtones of wilderness and its call to realign oneself spiritually (repent and believe the good news!), and those occasions when I was drawn to a particular psalm or piece of scripture, only to hear it read that day in Evening Prayer or used as a theme in the homily at Mass. In all of this the presence of God, leading and guiding, always intimately present, seemed so real. I felt cared for by God and experienced a renewed sense of calling to ministry. My only worry was that the spiritual disciplines of the monastery would dissipate when I returned to the parish. This turned out to be an ongoing struggle. In particular I realized that busyness feeds my ego, protects me from loneliness and facing the painful realities of a church in crisis, and is the seedbed from which acedia once again can grow in me. I also found it hard to maintain a spiritual life in the absence of some form of community or group support.

The Worth experience left me fascinated by the concept of acedia, and how insidiously and unconsciously it works itself into one's life. I developed a hunch that it is something that not only affected me but that it is a serious pandemic among clergy today. Underneath so much of the unhealthy dynamics in ministry and church life, such as burnout, cynicism, addiction, loneliness, and the formation of models of church and ministry focussed more on management than service, may be lurking the ancient 'demon' of acedia. The invidious problem is that most clergy have never heard the word 'acedia' and consequently are unaware of its dynamics.

Conclusion: Acedia Today

A reading of the literature makes it clear that acedia is not just confined to clergy and religious. Kathleen Norris, in *Acedia & Me* is clear that acedia potentially affects anyone whose life's priorities are out of kilter or who does not take the spiritual life seriously (see Norris, 2008). At a broader level, writers such as Jamison contest that Western culture is suffering a 'catastrophic loss of understanding of the need for self-awareness leading to widespread acedia' (Jamison, 2008, 55). He argues, 'spiritual carelessness seems ... to underlie much contemporary unhappiness' (Jamison, 2008, 57). This is an argument strongly made by writers such as Snell in *Acedia and its Discontents* (Snell, 2015). He argues that contemporary life is marked by metaphysical boredom despite the fact that we live in what he calls 'an empire of desire', in the subtitle of his book.

It is my belief that the word acedia needs to be reclaimed and defined and used to diagnose and describe the spiritual malaise common today in the lives of clergy, and more generally within the culture of the Christian Church/institution and secular society. Notwithstanding the broader usefulness of acedia for thinking about society more generally, as a Catholic diocesan priest it is my intention to focus in this study on the lives of Irish Catholic clergy, and to suggest that insights and findings might be applied to clergy of other parts of the Catholic Church as well as other Christian denominations. I would hope as we progress in this paper that seeking to articulate a working definition of the contemporary characteristics of acedia will aid diagnosis and a description of remedy which will enhance the spiritual and hence pastoral and personal lives of clergy ministering in these early years of the twenty-first century. However, an obsession with spending too much time trying to describe acedia can divert from what I see as more pressing and sometimes a missing issue in contemporary literature, namely what triggers acedia, and what spirituality, post-acedia, might look like.

2. ACEDIA AND CONTEMPORARY PRIESTHOOD

Introduction
In exploring the causes of my own spiritual malaise outlined in chapter one, I identified with the general consensus that Irish priesthood and the church in general is experiencing crisis (Conway, 2013a, 17; Nwobi, 2012, xi), uncertainty (Maloney, 2013; Conway, 2013a, 15 and 17), and grief (Zullo, 2001; Ranson, 2009). However this exploration did not of itself provide a clear insight into how my spiritual and ministerial life might be different. A transformative connection only occurred in my own experience at Worth Abbey during my sabbatical when Abbot Christopher Jamison diagnosed acedia. This ancient temptation offered a descriptive theological reflection of what was happening for me spiritually and professionally as I tried to live with the stresses and changes of contemporary ministry. It also offered the possibility of transformation in that writers, ancient and contemporary, have described remedies for acedia. It was in these early explorations of acedia that I first realized the potential for using this ancient tradition as a way of understanding the experiences of spiritual malaise among Irish Catholic clergy today and to begin to think also about ways towards transformation. It is this potential of acedia, as both diagnosis and remedy for clergy today, that I will explore in this chapter.

The Context in which Priests Live and Minister: Triggers of Acedia
Theologies of priestly spirituality have always been contextualized. I immediately recognized that this was important in terms of my approach to understanding contemporary clergy theologies of priesthood and the difficulties they experienced in living priesthood. While Conway concludes from his study of many books on priesthood written since the Second Vatican Council that 'what they all had in common was a sense that the priesthood was and still is in crisis' (Conway, 2013a, 17), there is a dearth of qualitative research which focusses on clergy experiences of priestly life and ministry, and

14

particularly the obstacles to spiritual development. In order to try to fill that gap, I used the following existing reflections as starting and departure points for developing an approach to research that would allow for a thick description and understanding of priestly experience and spirituality and the challenges to developing a spiritual life to emerge. This study does not assume that these sources wholly describe the context in which clergy live their priesthood today but they do provide a starting point that can help us to understand contemporary priesthood more clearly in an Irish context and what might trigger acedia.

Secularization and Detraditionalization

According to Michael Conway, 'significant changes at the level of culture are changing the very dynamics of faith and belief in society ... this is having an enormous impact on ministry' (2014, 132). Conway engages with two main analysts of the challenging effects of secularization on religious life in his study, and they are Charles Taylor and Lieven Boeve. Taylor, in writing about the 'social imaginary', suggests that 'what we are dealing with in the West is best understood ... as a radically transformed cultural context where the impact of the whole of technology, science, philosophy, rationality, and religion as well, is more than the sum of the parts' (Conway, 2013b, 388). Secularization therefore means 'the emergence of a complex set of conditions in our culture ... that leads us to understand, relate and respond to religion in ways that can truncate or short-circuit authentic religious experience' (cited in Conway, 2013b, 388). This research, therefore, explores the degree to which the characteristics of secularization, as described by Taylor, have had an influence on clergy identity and ministry in Ireland as a society that has secularized both rapidly and recently.

Secularization, using Boeve's categories of 'detraditionalisation' and pluralism, further informed my approach to research with clergy. He suggests that religious traditions, as living embodiments and communities of faith, no longer steer the process of constructing people's personal or religious identity (Boeve, 2005, 104–107). Conway suggests that priests are influenced by detraditionalization so that effectively detraditional practices influence how we do ministry and live priesthood (Conway, 2013b, 396). The research was thus framed in order to explore the extent to which this is true and how this process of detraditionalization impacts on priestly identity and spirituality in Ireland today. This process, again, has been rapid and recent, with clergy and the church operating with models of ministry that are, in my view, often no longer fit for purpose in such a radically changing society as twenty-first century Ireland.

Challenges to Priestly Spirituality

Maloney lists six specific pressures facing contemporary Irish clergy, namely increased workload and consequent role ambiguity, loneliness and isolation, the fallout from the sex abuse scandals, difficulties prioritising and sustaining a prayer life in the midst of increased work, a lack of support structures (and perceived poor leadership), and the impact of secularization (2013). Nwobi proposes poor formation as a principal factor of the crisis in priesthood today (2012). The language of crisis is used among many others, including by Conway, Kasper and Rahner (Conway, 2013b, 393), while Zullo suggests that priestly and church life is marked by liminality and the dynamics of transition. He describes liminality as that period in the middle of a transition when 'long held assumptions and beliefs begin to lose their power over our lives, and we are confronted with nothing to put in their place' (Zullo, 2001, 20). Grief is seen as necessary and normal in order to move out of liminality (Conway, 2013a, 15).

In the absence of any extant qualitative testing, I wanted to investigate the extent to which these conclusions about the pressures facing clergy accurately describe the experience of Irish priests – from *their* perspective – while also wanting to explore what other possible factors might be influential in their struggles. Interestingly none of the above authors mention acedia as a possible theological lens to understanding obstacles to spiritual growth, although they do focus on the challenges facing clergy. However, in this paper and in my own experience, acedia was more than a tool for diagnosing a problem, which is what most existing literature on the subject currently does. I also argue, as was the practice of the early eremitic monks, that clergy have to find ways of moving beyond the experience of acedia to a place of spiritual renewal.

Acedia and Priesthood: Diagnosing Acedia

As outlined in chapter one, Evagrius understood acedia to be a form of spiritual sloth, an avoidance of what was essential to the religious and spiritual life (namely spiritual disciplines and obedience to the demands of the Christian calling) in response to, as well as leading to, a questioning of the meaning of the monastic life. The triggers to acedia were hinted at in his use of the metaphor – the 'noonday demon' – to describe the condition. Other key writers from the fourth to the thirteenth centuries provided nuanced and contextual definitions of acedia. For instance, Aquinas saw acedia as a form of sorrow at not being in relationship with God because of the burden of commitment (DeYoung, 2004, 20). Earlier in my doctoral work, I compiled a list of definitions and symptoms of contemporary experiences of acedia from studying both ancient and medieval sources, and these definitions will be outlined in chapter three.

Distinctions in definition and theological understanding stem from etiological problems with the word acedia but also suggest, as I argue here, that the word can be contextualized for a contemporary audience, namely Catholic diocesan priests in Ireland. This is in line with McCarthy's assertion that one role of practical theology is to find a bridge between ancient traditions and present living reality (McCarthy, 2012, 198). Given the absence of reflections on acedia in light of the understandings of priestly experiences outlined above, these ancient traditions of acedia provide a theological lens for understanding low morale, burnout, forms of spiritual malaise, and barriers to spiritual development in clergy.

With the exception of monasticism, acedia was lost in the Christian spiritual tradition after Aquinas. In the last two decades there has been a flourishing of literature applying the deadly sin tradition to contemporary Christian life. This work, clearly influenced by the work of Evagrius, Cassian and Aquinas includes, Heher (2004), DeYoung (2004, 2009), Funk (2005), Finnegan (2008), Jamison (2008), Norris (2008), Tilby (2009), Reno (2011), Pope Francis (2013) and Rolheiser (2014). As well as contributing to the symptomology of acedia, these writers make important connections with other disciplines, particularly modern social science and positive psychology (Seligman, 2011; Gaffney, 2011) and, in doing so, uncover a number of behavioural, cognitive and affective symptoms of acedia.

Drawing on these works, a contemporary understanding of the condition for our purposes here, and in response to the Irish context and challenges facing priests in Ireland is, *'a loss of taste or lack of care for the spiritual life, or some aspect of it, which develops and persists within priests and the church as institution' leading eventually to questioning both the meaning of the spiritual life and priesthood*. It is also my contention in line with this tradition, that acedia can be remedied by lifestyle changes and virtuous living, hence the hopeful intervention of understanding spiritual crisis and priestly challenges in light of a theology of acedia. The above working definition and symptomology of acedia provides a lens for understanding spiritual malaise among clergy in the rest of this paper.

Conclusion: The Possibility of Remedying Acedia

In contemporary times, I believe a major instigator and reason for the persistence of acedia, often unconsciously, is the lack of a clear spirituality of priesthood and ecclesiology. Living through the crisis of a changing church, one's identity can be eroded. The transformation that acedia invites clergy to is nothing less than the embrace of a mature spiritual identity, and new ways of understanding priesthood and church. This shift, I argue, can only occur if the consistent advice to stay in one's cell, to stay awake, is heeded. This invitation is to live a reflective life, staying with the uncomfortable, painful feelings, grieving, waiting, allowing experience to shape a more mature spiritual identity and church, rather than ego needs that are more characteristic of a search for oneself and maintaining the institution, than any real search for God. Beaudoin describes the vocation of the post-modern theologian as a 'witness to dispossession' (Beaudoin, 2008).

Authentic spirituality, post-acedia, can only emerge from courageously embracing liminal dispossession. 'Staying with' teaches that meaning in life, well-being and flourishing is ultimately not about hedonistic happiness but is eudonistic and virtue based. I have suggested that a key virtue necessary for dealing with acedia today, and for flourishing during times of crisis and change, is resilience (McAlinden, 2013). The fruit of active resilience is beautifully described as hope in Romans 5:3–5. Resilience demands discipline; spiritual disciplines can become a burden and in themselves a trigger of acedia. Somehow life-giving spiritual disciplines and practices, and acedic remedies, need to shape the lives of clergy rather than them being yet another thing they have to do. Having attempted to provide a brief definition of acedia for the purposes of this paper, I now turn to describe the research I conducted with Catholic priests in Ireland on both their experiences of, and remedies for, acedia.

3. RESEARCHING ACEDIA

Introduction

Having explored the origins of acedia in the eremitic tradition, its significance for understanding my own condition and need for a renewed spirituality, and its usefulness for wider discourses about the experiences of clergy in Ireland, I now turn to outline my approach to researching this topic. Rooted in the principles of practical theology, I wanted to listen carefully and attentively to the voices of priests in Ireland so that my theology of acedia could be both rooted in, and be transformative of, lived human experience. I have noted that no qualitative study has to this point focussed on clergy experiences of acedia, or on the effects of crisis on the spiritual lives of contemporary Irish priests. I determined, therefore, to qualitatively investigate the spiritual lives of Irish Catholic clergy, especially forms of spiritual malaise and barriers to spiritual development which they experience, and the extent to which acedia provides a theological lens for understanding such issues and possibly transforming them.

Practical Theology as Methodology

Pierre Hadot makes the point that Christianity, especially in the monastic movements, 'was also considered as a *philosophia*, as a way of life that sought to live according to the paths of divine Wisdom' (Veling, 2011, 36). Eileen Charry likewise argues that classical Christian theology was more concerned with helping believers flourish and live a virtuous life than with proclaiming doctrine (1997, 19). For the early monks, prayer and theology, experience and practice were indistinguishable (Thompson, 2008; Green, 2009). Perhaps this is why Evagrius has been called the first practical theologian (Gagey, 2010, 80). Such an understanding of practical theology undergirds this paper. In that sense I see practical theology as a spiritual and sacramental discipline in that reflexive attention to the contemporary reality of priestly life reveals the presence of the Spirit in the midst of it and invites the Vatican II command to discern God's will by reading the signs of the times (*Gaudium et Spes*, 4). The goal of such practical theology is a more flourishing life, or in Veling's perhaps exaggerated claim, the 'transformation of the self' (Veling, 2011, 36), of practice (Graham, 2000) and ultimately of the Church.

Such a description of practical theology is empowering in that it considers reflection on the life experiences and discernment of clergy to be exercises in doing theology. Clergy in this study are, therefore, not simply the objects of study, but are also engaging in theology and, with me, are participants in the process of creating theology. Practical theology is the 'reintegration' of theology into life (Veling, 2005, 3) that leads to a better existence for human beings, or as Wolfteich concludes, 'the basic task that orients practical theology is to promote faithful discipleship' (2012, 330).

Located within practical theology, therefore, the specific methodology used in this study is what Graham et al. call 'Theology-in-Action'. The underlying principle of this approach to theology is that orthopraxis is central and the ultimate goal of theological discourse (2005, 170). This approach allows for a synthesis or triangulation of methods and the generation of conversations with various partners which are critical, interrogative, reflexive, contextual, dynamic and strategic (ibid. 2005, 6; Mason, 2002, 32). It is a methodology that celebrates and takes seriously the richness, depth, nuance, context, multi-dimensionality and complexity of social, ministerial and spiritual worlds. These experiences and beliefs serve as a context for the critical development of theological understanding (Graham, Walton and Ward, 2005, 6) so that theological reflection offers, in sync with my own philosophy of practical theology, a kind of practical wisdom, a way of living discipleship wisely.

Pattison's metaphor for the process of theological reflection, namely 'critical conversation' (Pattison, 2000, 136) is particularly useful here. In line with this understanding, personal reflection on my own experience will involve a conversation focussed on: the spiritual lives of clergy, the causes and experiences of spiritual malaise and barriers to spiritual development, an investigation about how acedia might be considered a theological lens for understanding spiritual difficulties, and conclusions. The conversation partners will be clergy, existing literature and discourses on acedia, a multi-disciplinary critique of the conditions that affect spiritual development as well as a critical appraisal of the experience of the researcher.

Pattison notes that the type of critical conversation which best constitutes theological reflection is structured and semi-formal (Pattison, 2000, 140). Consequently this research involved both autoethnography as well as in-depth semi-structured interviews with clergy. While a questionnaire might have been considered, acedic clergy would presumably have been 'careless' about returning surveys. Also a rich description of clergy's spiritual experience was more likely to be derived from interviewing. Further, the difficulties regarding the definition of acedia, and the fact that it can look like other conditions, required a more probing and exploratory form of investigation that allowed me to work with participants to talk through and explore acedia. This methodology is also pastoral in its approach in that it wanted to take human life seriously and attend seriously (Osmer, 2008, 57) to the experiences of clergy in face to face conversation.

In modern and contemporary times, developmental psychology and spirituality offer much academic reflection about assumed stages of spiritual progress (Fowler, 1996; Gilligan, 1990; Whitehead and Whitehead, 1999; Slee, 2004; Rolheiser, 2014). Mindful that spiritual progression is more complex and nuanced than stage models sometimes suggest, these discourses were nonetheless formative in the developing of an approach to research which sought to allow clergy to qualitatively explore their own spiritual growth, theologies of ministry and raison-d'être of priesthood, and to focus particularly on hindrances and challenges to spiritual development as well as disciplines for transforming crises and spiritual difficulties. I now turn to explain my methods for conducting this research.

Approaching the Qualitative Research

Incorporating my own experience (recorded in a reflective journal) and social context into the research was an important first step into the research. Etherington calls this approach to reflexive writing 'autoethnography' (2005, 139). Moschella considers autoethnography useful 'for practical theologians who wish to understand the complexity and nuances of human communities as they practice their spiritual faith' (2012, 232). She calls ethnography a form of 'prayerful beholding and attentiveness' and a way of seeing self and participants as primary theologians (Moschella, 2012, 227). All of this is central to my own understanding of practical theology as reflexive, sacramental, empowering and paving the way for spiritual growth and transformation. Hence, in terms of autoethnographic data collection, I have harvested all references to behavioural, cognitive and affective symptoms that I have experienced and/or noted in a journal I kept over several years, as well as my attempts to define acedia as a result of thinking about my own experience in light of literature on acedia. This data subsequently helped in the construction of interview questions while also providing personal insights into the experience of acedia and how to respond to it. As I developed the interview questions, I did so by trying to scrutinize any hermeneutical bias objectively vis-à-vis my own experience and assumptions, thereby avoiding the danger Morris expresses, 'that I read into dialogue partners what I want to read and ignore what I don't want to hear' (2014, 31). This writing of oneself into research is not unknown in social research (Mason, 2002, 45) and in practical theology, especially in theology that focusses on spirituality (Slee, 2004). Starting with one's own experience is commonly the impetus for developing an interest in research and it encourages reflexive interviewing.

In addition to my autoethonography, as I have already indicated, I also conducted interviews. The interviews involved thematic, topic-centred questions (Mason, 2002, 62). Hence clergy were firstly asked to identify the experiences of spiritual difficulties, malaise and burnout in their lives. This necessarily invited an exploration of participants' spiritual development and theologies of ministry and priesthood. Further questions explored the causes of spiritual difficulties and I explored with them the extent to which they felt their formation at seminary prepared them to face those difficulties. Probing questions were used with the intention of helping participants to differentiate the presence of acedia from other spiritual or psychological conditions. In relation to exploring acedia as a theological tool, participants were asked to consider the extent to which various behavioural, cognitive, and affective symptoms resonated with, or explained their experiences of, spiritual malaise. I used this list of characteristics, developed out of my own experience of acedia, and asked them to identify any which resonated with their own experiences:

- A lack of commitment or interest in prayer.
- A lack of interest in spiritual practices.
- Boredom or disillusionment with the spiritual life.
- Boredom or disillusionment with ministry.
- Loathing of one's situation or vocation.
- An ability to function but the heart is not really in ministry.
- Cynicism about faith, prayer, ministry, others.
- A sense that priesthood is growing into a specialty, giving of the self to specific others and not to others generally.
- Physical laziness.
- Being overly busy, but not necessarily with what is central to ministry and the spiritual life.
- A sense that life is becoming unmanageable and meaningless.
- Questioning vocation.
- Feeling discouraged.
- Feeling burned out.
- Sadness and/or depression.
- More focussed on management and maintenance than service.
- Overly materialistic, e.g. an over-emphasis on personal comfort, the need for constant holidays, or needing to have the latest gadget or car.
- Experiencing mid-life crisis.

Finally, in the last part of the interviews, in terms of thinking about transforming acedia, I was interested in discovering the extent to which priestly spirituality has matured in participants as obstacles and crises are experienced, as well as exploring the types of spiritual practices, disciplines and virtues that they have developed to support spiritual growth and meaning making.

As the study aimed to acquire in-depth information from a small group of people instead of drawing from a large representative sample of the entire population, I began with the intention of interviewing twelve priests and twelve spiritual directors who work with clergy. In the end, I was only able to interview eight priests, but their stories were rich, detailed and informative. Primarily I interviewed clergy colleagues who identify as experiencing some form of spiritual malaise. At clergy conferences where I presented my work, I also invited participants who resonate with spiritual malaise or acedia to be interviewed. In both cases purposeful sampling (Mason, 2002) and snowballing techniques ensured that eight research subjects were deliberately selected on the basis of their relevance to the research proposal.

Conclusion
It was hoped that these methods of recruiting could 'provide rich context bound information' (Creswell, 1994, 7) across age groups and various dioceses so that factors such as leadership in a particular place or date of ordination (for instance, before or after Vatican II) did not skew results. Interviews were recorded and transcribed by the researcher and participant's details were fully anonymized to protect their identity given the sensitive nature of the stories they shared with me. Generated data was subsequently analyzed by categorizing themes (Roulston, 2013, 153–75). The data was very rich and there was so much there but from it, two key areas emerged that will form the focus of the next two chapters. The discussion that follows draws on both my autoethnography and the interviews with clergy just described. In exploring what I discovered, this paper also begins to map out some

tentative strategies and remedies for addressing the effects of acedia and to consider what spirituality, post-acedia, might be like.

4. FORMATION AND SPIRITUAL PRACTICES

Introduction

Both the prevention of, and remedy for, acedia were, in the eremitic tradition, rooted in a re-orientation to renewed spiritual practice. In this chapter, I will consider clergy experiences of formation and argue that many priests in this study felt ill-prepared by seminaries to face difficult theological questions and crises in ministry, often leading to acedic symptoms. Only because of those moments of crisis were many forced to develop what is here called, alternative spiritual practices, to help them move beyond acedia and resource them to prevent acedic symptoms re-emerging later on. Below, in response to those experiences, ways in which understandings and practices of formation might be re-conceived will be addressed, while exploring the importance of ensuring through formation that priests have at their disposal a range of spiritual practices to enable the development of resilience for ministry.

Experiences of Formation

From the interviews, a broad definition and understanding of formation was articulated that has two key aspects to it. The first aspect is that priests spoke about and understood that their formation began in an early part of their lives. In particular, their experience of their church community was one of the things that most inspired them as young people to want to be a part of the Church and to serve Christ in the Church. Regular attendance at mass, participation in the rites and rituals of the Church, being a part of a local community, feeling a part of a communion of saints, being involved in church life from an early age were all very important in shaping these young people to want to give their lives to Christ in priestly ministry. In addition to the practices of the local church and participation in them, the ritual and practice of love and prayer in the home was also important as a tool for developing young people in such a way that Christ, the Church and priesthood were an attractive part of everyday life. Interviewees mentioned teachers, nuns, parents, grandparents, congregation members and priests who had, through their love and care, through their godly example, through their commitment to Christ, served as inspirations for exploring a vocation to priestly life. What the priests demonstrated and articulated was the need not to underestimate the role and importance of the local church and ordinary members of the churches in forming them – priests, religious and laity.

The second aspect of formation relates to the formation of seminary and the extent to which that has served priests well in preparing them with the tools they would need to sustain them in the face of the realities of priestly life. A number of interviewees spoke positively about the intellectual preparation of their seminary and that the theology was stimulating and engaging and rigorous and, for some, engagement in those activities could be enjoyable. The deep-rooting of priests in the theology and the tradition of the church should remain an important and central part of priestly formation as it can often be from the wisdom and insights of those who have gone before us that we learn how to meet some of the challenges that are ahead of us. It was, however, providing priests with skills to engage this wisdom with the realities of their ministries that was, for many, lacking. In addition, the community life of the seminary and the patterns of daily mass and prayers were often a positive experience during the years spent in college and for learning about the importance of the discipline and practice of prayer within the community. What was clear however for many of the participants, not all but certainly most, was that a predominant focus on this approach to spiritual practices that worked in an institution and in a community with others did not prepare priests well for the profound isolation and loneliness of the presbytery and parish afterwards.

In chapter five, this problem of priestly isolation and loneliness will be explored in much greater detail, but suffice to say here how inadequate these learned spiritual practices can be in ministry. In the experience at Worth, outlined in chapter one, the command to pray was easier to obey in the context of the Abbey with a supportive community around, all orientated towards one common focus, coming together corporately for spiritual nourishment regularly each day. As I had anticipated, it was much more difficult to continue this again on my own when faced with a daily workload that seemed impossible to complete, a sense of a lack of purpose in my life, and feeling undervalued by the institution of which I was a part. The context of parish ministry, and many other contexts of ministry in which priests now work, rarely replicates the experience of the seminary. Such new contexts of ministry, not least given that many priests now live and work alone as a result of declining numbers entering priesthood, demand a different preparation in a range of diverse spiritual practices that will sustain priests in the long term.

Formation is Corporate and Collective

Formation remains and has the potential to be crucial in terms of the well-being of clergy. It is important, therefore, to begin to think differently about formation and to consider how formative practices might be developed and improved. This begins with the understanding that the whole church has a part to play in priestly formation because, what has become clear, is that it is not something that happens only during the five or six years spent in seminary, but rather the shaping of young people, including priests, begins at a much earlier age. It begins in the home, in schools, in local parishes, and all kinds of people inspire children and teenagers to respond to Christ's invitation to priestly vocation and they do so through their holy lives and good example: priests, teachers, religious, parents, members of congregations and many others. Because each member of the Church has the potential to shape young people in this way, it is a sobering reminder that even without necessarily knowing or realizing it, that as we encounter other people in our daily lives, each one of us, we have the capacity to inspire others into a deeper relationship with Christ, and into a life of faithful discipleship. As a result, the whole Church has a huge responsibility for its young people, to care for them, to ensure the Church is a place of safety and love, and a place that equips them with the spiritual resources they will need to respond to the crises that may confront them at any point in their lives.

It is not just in the early years of life or at the seminary, however, that formation occurs but the whole of life has the potential to be a life in which the person is shaped more and more into the likeness of God. The concept of *theosis*, particularly important in the thinking of St Athanasius and St Irenaeus, is important in Eastern Orthodox thinking about salvation, but has been gaining in significance once again in Western thought. This way of thinking about salvation is rooted both in theologies of the incarnation and in concepts of *imago dei*. It is rooted in the incarnation because the separation between human and divine is overcome when God becomes a human being, one of us and one with us in the person of Jesus Christ. As God becomes like us so the possibility of humans becoming like God is opened up. *Theosis* is rooted in *imago dei* because, as Bartos (2006, 136) argues, we must understand that while being in the image of God is first and foremost a gift that belongs to every human person, each person is tasked with the mission of growing ever more into the likeness of God, priests and laity alike. This way of thinking understands salvation and, it is argued here, formation as a process and as a discipline of *becoming* that takes practice and hard work and that it is a lifelong enterprise for everyone.

However, being formed into the likeness of God begs the question what is God like and how should we strive towards that possibility? The answer to the first part of that question has been, in the Christian tradition, that God is Trinity – a communion of persons united in love in one substance. Kallistos Ware explains that, 'salvation is social and communal more particularly because of our faith in the Holy Trinity' (Ware, 1996, 68). In other words, we become more like God by modelling our lives ever more on the life of the Trinitarian God, by recognizing that we are only ever fully ourselves when we are fully in relationship with others and with God (drawing on Morris, 2014, 122–23). Such a notion is echoed in Pope Francis' Encyclical, *Laudato Si* (2015), where he extends this notion of interdependence to

30

the whole creation: 'God's goodness could not be represented fittingly by any one creature. Hence we need to grasp the variety of things in their multiple relationships … When we can see God reflected in all that exists, our hearts are moved to praise the Lord for all his creatures and to worship him in union with them.'

This understanding of salvation in relation to formation is important as a reminder of two key things: First, that formation, priestly or otherwise, is a process of *becoming* that happens throughout life and not just in seminary or beforehand – even if seminary can be valuable in preparing priests better for that life of *becoming*. Second, it reminds us that formation for all of us is a collective and collaborative exercise in which we participate in the formation of one another in order to corporately become more like God the Holy Trinity. In their own lives, priests in this study recognized the importance of the whole people of God in their formation and that formation itself is a lifelong process. What is also suggested here and will be further developed in chapter five is that the whole Church of God, every member, has a role to play in sustaining clergy in times of crisis and helping them to avoid or overcome acedic symptoms. This points towards a spiritual practice for the Church that recognizes the interdependence of laity and clergy for their collective common good and well-being.

Formation and Alternative Spiritual Practices
Seminaries are concerned with preparing ordinands for the priestly life, giving them the resources to support and sustain them for the whole of life. Many of the participants felt they had been given good intellectual resources at seminary with a strong foundation in theological, historical, biblical and philosophical training. However, many felt they lack the reflective and reflexive skills to be able to engage those intellectual resources of the faith with the realities of life in parishes. The discipline of practical theology and its methodologies of theological reflection have been widely used in universities and centres of ministerial preparation for many years in a variety of Christian traditions. Research shows that the quality of the teaching of

31

practical theology is often patchy at best and that the understanding of, and ability of students to use, theological reflection by those in ministry is also varied (Thompson, 2008). However, theological reflection taught well and learned as a discipline for life has the potential to be an important resource for clergy that seminaries could equip their students to use more effectively. It brings the resources of the faith tradition, the wisdom of those who have gone before us, into 'critical conversation' with the hard and difficult questions that priests can face on a daily basis. The opening chapters of John Swinton's book, *Raging with Compassion* (2003), provide a brilliant example of the difficult questions that priests may have to grapple with, and why having the skills to reflect on them is so important for themselves and the people among whom they serve. If priests are to be resourced better for the challenges and realities of their daily ministry in the future, having this skill to help them will be crucial.

Further, as we have seen, many priests found that the patterns of prayer learned and practiced in seminary, while suitable for the seminary, were not often useful for ministry afterwards. Consequently many had discovered alternative ways of praying, of being energized, of connecting with God, of being immersed in the love of Christ, but these had been 'discovered', not taught, stumbled upon later in life when it seemed as though what had been taught and learned in seminary was not doing what it should. Perhaps one of the challenges for seminary formation for the future would be to find space to explore multiple spiritual practices that involve those traditionally taught like the office, saying mass, and so forth, but include also introducing seminarians to some of those alternative practices that priests have subsequently developed in their ministries. As a result, when new priests go into parish, they would be aware of a range of different possible ways of living, moving and having their being in Christ that enables them to be resilient in their daily lives. In other words, let us learn from these experiences of priests today, and what they have discovered has been useful to them in their ministries, to form and prepare the priests of the future better for parish life.

Such alternative spiritual practices that priests had developed included lighting a candle and praying or meditating on that as a focus, seeing the mass both as a prayer that nourishes the priest as well as a ritual that is offered for the people. Others found walks by the sea or in the hills as important times of spiritual practice to connect with the self and with God, while some wrote poetry, others were sustained by writing more generally. Some found preaching was a way into prayer, some said the daily office, some talked of learning to see God in nature or in people, others talked about practicing mindfulness, some used pilgrimage as a way into prayer, others reading spiritual texts, and, finally, some found nourishment in the ancient prayers and traditions of Ireland. This is a long list of varying and diverse practices that provides a starting point for opening up to seminarians a variety of spiritual practices and ways of praying that may sustain them in ministry early on in their training and throughout their lives, rather than having to discover something out of necessity because of being confronted with a particular crisis. Seminaries could never prepare everyone for every eventuality. We are all different, and who we are shapes the kinds of things that will help to sustain us and enable us to flourish, but perhaps if more of these multiple ways of living a spiritual life could be experienced in seminary, priests would be equipped better when they find themselves experiencing acedic symptoms.

Conclusion
St Paul taught us that we should 'pray without ceasing' (1 Thessalonians 5:17), which suggests that the whole of life and all that we do in life can be an expression of prayer and each moment forms us more and more into who we are as we journey together into becoming more in the likeness of God. The whole of life is a process of formation and consequently the whole Church has a responsibility to ensure the well-being of its priests, as well as one another and the rest of creation. The role of the whole people of God in forming and sustaining priests has always been a part of the practice of the Church and the interviews showed how much this was valued by those in Holy Orders. This chapter

has also argued that the importance of training both in reflective and reflexive skills for ministry where priests have the capacity and tools to connect the everyday with the wisdom of the past, and multiple patterns of spiritual practices, need to be priorities for those delivering seminary training in the future. This broad understanding of formation and its implications, together with these specific recommendations for seminaries are crucial for the sake and well-being of priests and for the whole Church.

5. WELL-BEING, RELATIONSHIPS AND COMMUNITY

Introduction
With the numbers of priests leaving seminary and the numbers of people attending church dropping radically over the past two decades, the pressure on priests to take on more work and to maintain the existing structures that were more suitable for an earlier period of history has been particularly problematic. The ensuing loneliness and isolation caused by fewer priests more widely dispersed, added to by a vow of celibacy, has led to sense of clergy feeling under-valued, under-supported, lonely, and focussed much more on management and maintenance of an institution than on faithful service and witness to Christ. The interviews I conducted inform and reinforce what has been stated above and, in response, this chapter will consider how the Catholic Church in Ireland might learn from its own experiences and the practices of other professions and organizations, to support its clergy better, and focus on a future for itself that is orientated towards a faith that is life-giving for the whole Church, priests included.

Workload and Well-Being
When most of the participants in this study were ordained, be it twenty or thirty years ago, the general expectation and experience was that they would spend their ministries working in a parish with a team of other priests. More recently, however, with a significant decrease in numbers of those entering seminaries over the past two decades, the likelihood that a priest is now working as part of a larger team is much reduced. In addition, the work that needs to be done in dioceses has not decreased at the same pace, but has rather stayed at the same levels or even increased. The pressures this puts on many priests to cover the same volume of work with fewer people is immense, leading to a sense of often being overly busy, but not necessarily with what is central to ministry and the spiritual life. Many other acedic symptoms were evident in the way priests spoke about their ministry in that there

was a clear sense that life had become unmanageable and meaningless. Others felt burned out, discouraged, sad or depressed, and that their role had become one of management and maintenance of an institution in decline rather than genuine loving service and faithful witness to God's people. All of this suggests acedia. In order to get things done, some described working from the moment of rising in the morning to going to bed at night, finding only time for one's self and time for spiritual practices to nourish ministry by getting up especially early or staying up very late. Living in a parish, living, as it were, 'on the job', often meant that these were the only times a priest had available to escape from the pressures of the role and to find space to care for the self.

Linked to rising workloads as a result of decreasing numbers of priests, was a sense of frustration with the institution of the Church and its hierarchies that seemed not to be supporting priests. Many expressed a sense of feeling uncared for by the institution, that when priests were struggling or unable to cope, nobody seemed to be interested or willing to help. Some felt stressed because they found themselves in roles they were not suited to doing, and it was explained how too often the appropriateness of the person to the role they were being asked to take on by their bishop was rarely considered in making appointments. Frustration with the institution was also expressed because it was felt that current models of ministry that had worked well in the past were no longer suited to the present. With a changing society and a changing role of the church in that society, together with fewer priests to do the work, models of ministry need to change, it was said, to those that involve a greater role for lay people. The institution needs to exercise more leadership in addressing this reality and to take responsibility for it in order to protect the well-being of clergy and make the future life of the Church for all people sustainable. This would need training for lay people, a possible adjustment in their expectations of clergy, and investment from the institution to foster lay learning and that change in culture. In that sense, remedying acedia is, to a large extent, the responsibility of the hierarchies of the Church to recognize that smaller numbers of priests cannot do everything and that there has to be an environment created in which priestly well-being is fostered and becomes a much higher priority in strategic planning and decision-making.

Acedia, Loneliness and Relationships

Another major contributor to a lack of priestly well-being, experienced by participants and many other priests too, is a sense of profound loneliness. This was by far one of the biggest factors affecting clergy well-being and prompting acedic symptoms. An aspect of this has been alluded to already in that priests who would often have worked with and lived together with other priests in community twenty or thirty years ago, often find themselves now working and living alone. The isolation of the presbytery and the loneliness it nurtures is exacerbated by the way that the understanding of the role of the priest within the communities in which they are located can also often lead to a sense of feeling alone. One participant talked about how historic understandings of the role of the priest in relation to the laity can leave the priest feeling separate or set apart from the people among whom he is serving. Some spoke about how having time with friends often demanded a lot of arranging in advance as getting to them involved planning ahead and sometimes the need to travel some distance. Another explained that while priests were often with other people in the parish for a considerable amount of time, they still often felt quite isolated. One mentioned, for example, how they are never invited round to someone's house for a cup of tea or out to the pub for a pint because they were a person others wanted to 'spend time with'. Rather, it was perceived that they were invited out because they were the priest. In other words, it was their role that was the source and reason for relationships within a community rather than the priest sensing that members of their communities wanted to spend time with them as a human being, as a distinct person, or as a friend.

Overwhelmingly, however, loneliness was exacerbated most of all by rules around celibacy and relationships. A number spoke about how they had entered priestly life because it was one way of concealing their sexual identity. A number said how answering awkward questions about why they had not married or did not have children disappeared if you became a priest. Using priesthood as a means of concealment of sexuality often led to acedic symptoms such as sadness or depression, even sometimes addictive tendencies. That inability to be totally honest about who you are had been so damaging for some of the participants. Others spoke about going home to an empty house, the lack of someone to be 'intimate with', not necessarily in a sexual way, but someone who might give you a hug, tell you it would be OK, ask you how your day was, or sit and watch television together in silence. Some lamented also not being able to have children. For some the intimacy of a sexual relationship and the inability to fulfil their humanity in this embodied way had been a cause of profound hurt.

Obviously this is a much bigger issue for the Church than its particular manifestation and expression in Ireland, but the impact of loneliness, isolation, lack of intimacy in whatever form it had taken, had had serious effects on the well-being and, in some instances, the mental health of clergy. Pope Francis said, 'The human being aspires to love and to be loved. This is our deepest aspiration: to love and be loved; and definitively' (Pope Francis, 2014). This profound but unfulfilled longing to love and to be loved, truly loved, that is so crucial for all of our humanity, had led not only to mental health problems, but addictions to things such as alcohol, drugs or sex. Such loneliness, such profound hurt, such feelings that lead to the diminishment of the mind and body surely cannot be what God desires for any human person. Often it was not from, or within, the institution of the Church that the resources were found to address or help with any of this, but rather the Church itself was viewed as the source of this hurt and harm. Instead, priests had usually only found help by turning to friends, counsellors, psychotherapists or other professionals outside of the Church, and usually having to fund such support from their own personal finances.

Community and Relationships as Remedy for Acedia

In the discussion in chapter four, it was argued that our formation into the likeness of God is a collaborative and a collective exercise. One of the biggest challenges to ministry and priestly well-being today is feelings of profound loneliness and isolation. If all Christian persons have a collective responsibility to collaborate in the process of becoming like God, remedying the acedic effects of isolation and loneliness can perhaps be achieved by fostering a similar sense of collective and collaborative responsibility for one another, in particular priests among themselves, and also priests and laity together. Consequently, new ways of thinking about how priests are located in communities, what and who the priest is in relation to lay people, and how mutual relationships of love and care for all members of the Church, lay and clergy alike, need to be developed. On one level, we need a new theology of priesthood and of the laity. On another level, in practice, priests with local congregations and communities need to think about how a person placed there to serve and support a community is themselves supported by the community and enabled to become a part of that community. This may require investment in training and facilitation as well as a change in culture and attitude towards the role of the priest and who the priest is in relation to the laity.

Acedia and Celibacy

For some priests, one way to address the isolation and loneliness they experience would be through ending the vow of celibacy placed upon priests. Given how long celibacy has been a part of the Church's understanding of priesthood, it is not likely that this will change in the foreseeable future. However, the stresses this puts on clergy to conceal who they really are and to suppress this aspect of their humanity and the subsequent destructiveness this causes was very clear in the interviews. For the eremitic monks living with acedia, an important remedy was to find ways of being able to stay in one's cell, to live with pain and suffering so as not to let it consume or destroy the person. Such an approach to the pain that the vow of celibacy causes, and the isolation and loneliness that is experienced because of it, is deeply problematic.

Suffering and pain is an inevitable part of human life and it is important that methods of coping with that in whatever forms it takes are developed, not least through appropriate spiritual practices. At the same time, suffering and pain and their destructive powers should never simply be tolerated and accepted but, wherever possible, should be challenged and transformed. It is important to note here, however, that developing resilience in the face of hurt and harm and seeking to transform the causes of such suffering are not mutually exclusive. Indeed both are crucial. This research encourages the institution of the Church to think anew about priesthood and celibacy in light of the destructive impact it has on its clergy. Priests and laity need to be a part of that movement for change if it is to be realized. However, in the shorter term, remedying acedic symptoms among priests will involve finding ways to learn to live with their current situation, to remain in the cell of celibacy, and to find ways of being resilient in the face of celibacy's challenges and not to let it overcome or destroy their humanity. This is hugely demanding and it is difficult to know how realistic or achievable such a proposition really is. But as long as the Church remains committed to its current practices on celibacy, priests in that Church must find ways of protecting their well-being and sustaining their humanity. The institution also has an important part to play in facilitating that as long as it maintains its current position on this matter.

Transforming Acedia in the Institution

Mitigating isolation and loneliness might involve the Church's hierarchy in better facilitating clergy in their support of one another. It is normal practice in professions like counselling, that regular supervision takes place with an experienced practitioner detached from the practice of the counsellor (BACP, 2016a, 2016b). Having someone to go to in order to talk things through and unload burdens is of paramount importance. In many ways, spiritual direction helps with this but this could perhaps be more structured, even compulsory for priests, and involve fully trained and experienced spiritual directors. This is not about adding another burden on to priests, but learning about the importance of developing structures and systems that support and foster well-being (BACP, 2016a, 13).

In certain times of crisis, if a priest needs particular help, for example, with depression or another mental health problem, drawing on the expertise of the psychotherapeutic professions would be beneficial and should be supported financially. In addition, structured, intentional, regular meetings of small groups of clergy for facilitated reflection on what is going on in parishes, with mutual support networks subsequently developed to work things through, could be beneficial in both preventing and remedying acedia. Facilitated intentional reflection on practice is regularly used in other professions and contexts. Again, this would require investment of time from clergy but also some investment of money from the Church.

Learning from Mistakes and Other Leadership Practices

Within parishes, priests are in a position of responsibility and oversight and the very nature of this role can lead to isolation. This kind of role and relationship with congregations is perhaps not unlike a management role in many other contexts which can themselves be quite isolating. In management, for example, certain boundaries have to be maintained so that it is difficult to confide in colleagues about everything because certain things have to be confidential. At times of crises, or if there is conflict between the institution and its employees, managers may find themselves stuck in the middle, totally isolated, without any support from their institution as well as from their colleagues, who at other times can so often be a source of inspiration and strength. At a time of crisis, the impact of that isolation can be very significant with serious costs to the person in leadership in terms of their health and well-being.[3] Many priests will recognize these difficulties in relation to

---

3   This reflection partly comes from reflections of the experience of Wayne Morris in a role of management and leadership in his own institution.

their own ministries and contexts. Further, clergy who are located in parishes, in positions of power, may feel isolated, in a constant process of boundary negotiation, and often caught between an institution and a community feeling as though they do not have any support from either.

The isolation that priests can feel in their communities because of the roles they have within them is not unique and it is important to learn from the experience of people in roles of leadership both inside and outside of the Church. We have enough experience in the academy, in contexts of professional practice outside of the Church, and within the Church itself, to know not to let every individual who is dealing with difficulties reach a point of personal crisis before a response is made and support is given. We know what causes pressures and strain: too much to do, competing demands, loneliness and isolation, caught between congregations and institution and yet, the same problems are repeated over and over, and the hurt and harm caused is replicated time and time again. It is time for the Church to learn from these mistakes and from practices in other contexts in order to find ways of ensuring clergy are better cared for and supported in parishes. Prevention is surely better than remedy and would be a sign of a Church that has become both reflective of, and reflexive on, its self.

Acedia and New Patterns of Ministry
A final challenge to priests and the Church in addressing acedia emerges out of the need to adapt patterns of ministry to something more suitable to the context of twenty-first century Ireland. Once again churches are not unique in finding themselves with fewer resources and fewer people to do jobs while also not wanting to let go of any aspect of the work it has always done. In addition, in times of declining resources, there is often pressure to consider developing new initiatives to ensure future sustainability and growth. However, doing the same activities with fewer resources contributes to burnout, a low sense of well-being, and, is ultimately exploitative. Given the decline in the numbers of priests and the desire to ensure that the Catholic Church

can flourish and grow in Ireland, there has to be an acknowledgement of the need for change and plans to manage it so as to sustain those who are ordained in the Church in the present. That may mean taking difficult decisions about what activities are priorities and what are not, while focussing on what is considered to be essential and letting go of what is not. If work is still not sustainable, then it is essential to find ways of adapting what is done. In the case of the Catholic Church in Ireland, that surely includes the greater use of lay people, many of whom are willing and able to take on a greater role. In *Share the Good News: National Directory for Catechesis* (Irish Catholic Bishops' Conference, 2011b), and *Grouping Parishes for Mission* (Irish Catholic Bishops' Conference, 2011a), and in the development of formation courses for lay leaders, the Irish Catholic Episcopal Conference has supported such a theology and ministry of participation. It is now time to put that into practice and make that theology a lived reality.

Conclusion

If the church wants to contribute to sustaining and supporting their clergy, deeper reflection on how to be the church in the future is essential. There is not space to further explore what this would look like in any more detail here and anyway, something so important should be done thoughtfully, prayerfully and carefully with bishops, priests, religious and laity collaborating together to consider what the Catholic Church of the future in Ireland will be like. In light of this research and what has been argued to this point, however, some guiding principles might include: the need to care for and ensure the well-being of priests and to develop structures to facilitate that; to develop new theologies of priesthood and laity that affirm both as equal collaborators in the future of the Church and to break down barriers that lead to a separation of clergy and laity; to invest in lay training and spiritual development; to prioritize activities and have the courage and discernment to determine what is less important and to let that go; and above all, to ensure the Church is a faithful and authentic witness to the love of Christ in all aspects of what it does, including in the care of its clergy.

6. CONCLUSION: SPIRITUALITY, PRIESTHOOD AND THE CHURCH POST-ACEDIA

This paper aims to contribute in some small way to thinking and practice about the future and well-being of priests in Ireland. Using acedia as a lens through which to think about priesthood and the Church in Ireland is ultimately about enabling flourishing at a time of crisis. Part of the way forward is rooted in the need to enable priestly resilience through spiritual practices, but focussing only on priestly resilience places the responsibility for responding to spiritual malaise too heavily on the shoulders of priests themselves. No doubt that has to be the case in part, but what has also been argued is that human flourishing is collaborative and collective and it is only when the whole church – laity, religious, priests, the hierarchy – recognizes the problems and commits to transformation that a real difference will be made.

In chapter three, a list of symptoms of acedia that priests may partially or wholly experience as part of their ministry was outlined. In chapters four and five, we have explored the reasons why acedia is experienced and how individuals, communities and the Church as a whole can help to prevent and/or remedy acedia. We have also learned that priests have developed resilience through alternative spiritual practices to sustain them in times of crises. But what might a spirituality post-acedia for priests of today, or even a spirituality pre-acedia for the priests of the future, look like? In conclusion, here are some of those characteristics:

- Being formed daily more and more into the likeness of Christ.
- A commitment to prayer.
- Daily engaging in a range of spiritual practices.
- Finding the spiritual life to be life-giving and sustaining for ministry.

- Having the spiritual resources to support moments of crisis or difficulty.
- Loving one's vocation and ministry.
- Loving the communities in which you serve.
- Having a heart fully focussed on ministry.
- Being available to and showing love and value to every human person.
- An energy for life.
- Loving one's self.
- Being in full and meaningful relationships with others.
- Being valued and loved because of who you are and not because of your role.

At this moment in the life of the Catholic Church in Ireland, these characteristics may seem like an ideal that can only be dreamed about but never actually realized. Such pessimism is perhaps reflective of the acedia that is so much a part of the life of the Church today. I would argue, however, that such goals are not unrealistic ideals, but the standards that priests should set ourselves, rooted in the belief that Christ always and everywhere seeks the very best for all of his people. May the priests of today, together with the laity and hierarchy of the Catholic Church in Ireland have both the courage and the vision to work towards such possibilities, inspired by Christ who loves each one of us so completely.

Bibliography

Amdt, W. F., & Gingrich, W. F. (1979). *A Greek-English Lexicon of the New Testament and Other Early Christian Literature*. Chicago, IL: University of Chicago Press.

Bartos, E. (2006). *Deification in Eastern Orthodox Theology*. Eugene, OR: Wipf and Stock.

Beaudoin, T. (2008). *Witness to Dispossession: The Vocation of a Postmodern Theologian*. New York, NY: Orbis Books.

Boeve, L. (2005). Religion after Detraditionalization: Christian Faith in a Post-Secular Europe, *Irish Theological Quarterly, 70*(2), 99–122

British Association of Counsellors and Psychotherapists. (2016a). *Ethical Framework for the Counselling Professions*. Lutterworth, UK: BACP.

British Association of Counsellors and Psychotherapists. (2016b). *A Registrant's Guide to Supervision*. Lutterworth, UK: BACP.

The Catholic Youth Bible Revised: New Revised Standard Version. (2005). Winona, MN: St Mary's Press.

Charry, E. T. (1997). By the Renewing of Your Minds: The Pastoral Function of Christian Doctrine. New York, NY: Oxford University Press.

Conway, E. (Ed.). (2013a). *Priesthood Today: Ministry in a Changing Church*. Dublin, Ireland: Veritas.

Conway, E. (2013b). 'With Reverence and Love': Being a Priest in a Detraditionalised Cultural Context. In *Irish Eucharistic Congress, 50th International Eucharistic Congress: Proceedings of the International Symposium of Theology* (382–98). Dublin, Ireland: Veritas.

Conway, M. (2014). Ministry in Transition. *The Furrow*, 65(3), 131–49.

Creswell, J. (1994). *Research Design: Qualitative and Quantitative Approaches*. Thousand Oaks, CA: SAGE Publications.

Crislip, A. (2005). The Sin of Sloth or the Illness of the Demons? The Demon of Acedia in Early Christian Monasticism. *Harvard Theological Review, 98*(2), 143–69.

DeYoung, R. K. (2004). Acedia's Resistance to the Demands of Love: Aquinas on the Vice of Sloth. *The Thomist, 68*(2), 39.

DeYoung, R. K. (2009). *Glittering Vices: A New Look at the Seven Deadly Sins and their Remedies*. Ada, MI: Brazos Press.

Etherington, K. (2005). *Becoming a Reflexive Researcher: Using Our Selves in Research*. London, UK: Jessica Kingsley Publishers.

Evagrius of Pontus. (1972). *The Praktikos & Chapters On Prayer* (J. E. Bamberger, Trans.). Trappist, KY: Cistercian Publications.

Evagrius of Pontus (2003). *The Greek Ascetic Corpus* (R. E. Sinkewicz, Trans.). Oxford, UK: Oxford University Press.

Evagrius of Pontus (2009). *Talking Back: A Monastic Handbook for Combating Demons* (D. Brakke, Trans.). Collegeville, MN: Liturgical Press.

Finnegan, J. (2008). *The Audacity of Spirit: The Meaning and Shaping of Spirituality Today*. Dublin, Ireland: Veritas.

Fowler, J. W. (1996). *Faithful Change: The Personal and Public Challenges of Postmodern Life*. Nashville, TN: Abingdon Press.

Francis. (2013). *The Joy of the Gospel: Evangelii Gaudium:* London, UK: Pauline Books & Media.

Francis. (2014). *Address of Pope Francis: Meeting with Young People of the Dioceses of Abruzzi and Molise.* http://w2.vatican.va/content/francesco/en/speeches/2014/july/documents/papa-francesco_20140705_molise-giovani.html

Francis, (2015). *Laudato Si': On Care for our Common Home.* http://w2.vatican.va/content/francesco/en/encyclicals/documents/papa-francesco_20150524_enciclica-laudato-si.html

Funk, M. M. (2005). *Thoughts Matter: The Practice of the Spiritual Life.* New York, NY: Continuum.

Gaffney, M. (2011). *Flourishing: How to Achieve a Deeper Sense of Well-being, Meaning and Purpose – Even When Facing Adversity.* Dublin, Ireland: Penguin Ireland.

Gagey, H.-J. (2010). Pastoral Theology as a Theological Project. In J. Sweeney, G. Simmonds, & D. Lonsdale (Eds.), *Keeping Faith in Practice: Aspects of Catholic Pastoral Theology* (80–98). London, UK: SCM Press.

Gilligan, C. (1990). *In a Different Voice: Psychological Theory and Women's Development.* Boston, MA: Harvard University Press.

Graham, E. (2000). Practical Theology as Transforming Practice. In J. Woodward, & S. Pattison (Eds.), *The Blackwell Reader in Pastoral and Practical Theology* (104–17). Oxford, UK: Blackwell Publishing Ltd.

Graham, E., Walton, H., & Ward, F. (2005). *Theological Reflection: Methods.* London, UK: SCM Press.

Green, L. (2009). *Let's Do Theology: Resources for Contextual Theology.* London, UK: Mowbray.

Harmless, W. & Fitzgerald, R. R. (2001). The Sapphire Light of the Mind: The *Skemmata* of Evagrius Ponticus. *Theological Studies, 62,* 498–529.

Heher, M. (2004). *The Lost Art of Walking on Water: Reimaging the Priesthood.* New York, NY: Paulist Press.

Irish Catholic Bishops' Conference. (2011a). *Grouping Parishes for Mission: An Exploration of Key Issues.* Dublin, Ireland: Veritas.

Irish Catholic Bishops' Conference. (2011b). *Sharing the Good News: National Directory for Catechesis.* Dublin, Ireland: Veritas.

Jamison, C. (2008). *Finding Happiness: Monastic Steps for a Fulfilling Life.* London, UK: Weidenfeld & Nicolson Ltd.

Maloney, G. (2013). A Look at a Priest's Life. *The Furrow, 64*(1), 10–16.

Mason, J. (2002). *Qualitative Researching*. London, UK: SAGE Publications.

McAlinden, M. (2013). Living Baptismally: Nurturing a Spirituality for Priestly Wellbeing. Unpublished article submitted to the University of Chester as part requirement for the degree of Doctor of Professional Studies in Practical Theology.

McCarthy, M. (2012). Spirituality in a Postmodern Era. In J. Woodward, & S. Pattison (Eds.), *The Blackwell Reader in Pastoral and Practical Theology* (192–206). Oxford, UK: Blackwell Publishing Ltd.

Morris, W. (2014). *Salvation as Praxis: A Practical Theology of Salvation for a Multi-Faith World*. London, UK: Bloomsbury Publishing.

Moschella, M. C. (2012). Ethnography. In B. J. Miller-McLemore (Ed.), *The Wiley-Blackwell Companion to Practical Theology* (1st ed., 224–33). Chichester, UK: Blackwell Publishing Limited.

Norris, K. (2008). *Acedia & Me: A Marriage, Monks, and a Writer's Life*. New York, NY: Riverhead Books.

Nwobi, P. (2012). *Poor Formation as a Principal Factor to the Crisis in Priesthood Today*. Bloomington, IN: AuthorHouse.

Osmer, R. R. (2008). *Practical Theology: An Introduction*. Grand Rapids, MI: William B. Eerdmans Publishing Company.

Pattison, S. (2000). Some Straw for the Bricks: A Basic Introduction to Theological Reflection. In J. Woodward & S. Pattison (Eds.), *The Blackwell Reader in Pastoral and Practical Theology* (135–45). Oxford, UK: Blackwell Publishing Ltd.

Ranson, D. (2009). *The Contemporary Challenge of Priestly Life: A Meditation on the Paschal Mystery*. New York, NY: Paulist Press.

Reno, R. R. (2011). *Fighting the Noonday Devil – and Other Essays Personal and Theological*. Grand Rapids, MI: William B. Eerdmans Publishing Company.

Rolheiser, R. (2014). *Sacred Fire: A Vision for a Deeper Human and Christian Maturity*. New York, NY: Image Books.

Roulston, K. (2013). *Reflective Interviewing: A Guide to Theory and Practice*. London, UK: SAGE Publications.

Seligman, M. (2011). *Flourish: A New Understanding of Happiness and Well-being – and How to Achieve Them*. London, UK: Nicholas Brealey Publishing.

Slee, N. (2004). *Women's Faith Development: Patterns and Processes*. Farnham, UK: Ashgate Publishing Ltd.

Snell, R. J. (2015). *Acedia and Its Discontents: Metaphysical Boredom in an Empire of Desire*. Ranchos de Taos, NM: Angelico Press.

Swinton, J. (2003). *Raging with Compassion: Pastoral Responses to the Problem of Evil*. Grand Rapids, MI: William B. Eerdmans Publishing Company.

Thompson, J. (2008). *Theological Reflection*. London, UK: SCM Press.

Tilby, A. (2009). *The Seven Deadly Sins: Their Origin in the Spiritual Teaching of Evagrius the Hermit*. London, UK: SPCK Publishing.

Veling, T. A. (2005). *Practical Theology: 'On Earth as It Is in Heaven'*. Maryknoll, NY: Orbis Books.

Veling, T. A. (2011). Catholic Practical Theology: Reflections on an Emerging Field. *Compass, 2*, 35–39.

Vogel, J. A. (2009). The Speed of Sloth: Reconsidering the Sin of *Acedia*. *Pro Ecclesia, XVIII*(1), 50–68.

Ware, K. (1996). *How Are We Saved? The Understanding of Salvation in the Orthodox Tradition*. Minneapolis, MN: Light and Life Publishing Company.

Wenzel, S. (1967). *The Sin of Sloth: Acedia in Medieval Thought and Literature* (2nd ed.). Chapel Hill, NC: The University of North Carolina Press.

Whitehead, E. E., & Whitehead, J. D. (1999). *Christian Life Patterns: The Psychological Challenges and Religious Invitations of Adult Life*. New York, NY: The Crossroad Publishing Company.

Wolfteich, C. E. (2012). Spirituality. In B. J. Miller-McLemore (Ed.), *The Wiley-Blackwell Companion to Practical Theology* (1st ed., 328–36). Chichester, UK: Blackwell Publishing Limited.

Zullo, J. (2001). Navigating Transitions. *The Works*, Winter 2001, 18–22.

RESPONSES

ACEDIA – MEMORY AND CONTEMPLATION: THE PAINTINGS IN THE COLLEGE CHAPEL

John-Paul Sheridan

Introduction

In 1983 Martin and I began our studies at St Patrick's College, Maynooth along with about sixty other seminarians. In the intervening years we had kept up with each other in various ways and had met on an annual basis at Lourdes. In an email in 2014 I told him that I was to begin on the staff at Maynooth in the area of Religious Education and Catechesis. He replied almost instantly and told me he was also starting at Maynooth in the area of Practical Theology. Those first months at Maynooth were memorable as we plotted to place our respective subjects (never truly respected among the other theological disciplines) at the centre of the Pontifical University. Sadly, this was never to be. Although Martin had begun to make strides in Practical Theology, his endeavours would be cut short by his untimely passing.

In long discussion regarding our respective research interests Martin had often spoken to me about acedia and his encounter with it. He spoke with passion about the importance of naming this spiritual malaise and how it was not just him who had experience of it. As he writes in the section, 'Acedia and My Vocation',

> I developed a hunch that it is something that not only affected me but that it is a serious pandemic among clergy today. Underneath so much of the unhealthy dynamics of ministry and church life, such as burnout, cynicism, addiction, loneliness, and the formation of models of church and ministry focussed more on management than service, may be lurking the ancient 'demon' of acedia. The invidious problem is that most clergy have never heard the word 'acedia' and consequently are unaware of its dynamics. (12)

This piece I offer is to honour my friend and colleague. It has been a long time coming. I spent a great deal of time trying to formulate what I might say. At table one day, another colleague suggested that my inability to commit to paper might be an indication that I was suffering from the same spiritual malaise about which Martin wrote so eloquently.

Six Paintings

Anyone who has visited the College Chapel at Maynooth cannot fail but to be overawed by the place. Its grandeur and decoration harken back to a different time and world. There is a touch of aspic about the place, as it seems somewhat frozen in time. What is not as obvious about the place is that two themes run through the decoration of nearly every space in the building. Firstly, *laus Deo* (the praise of God) and secondly, the symbols and images associated with a place dedicated to the education and formation of men for the priesthood. In its 220 or so years of existence, Maynooth has ordained nearly 11,000 priests for the home and foreign mission. Their portraits in the form of 'classpieces' grace the walls of the cloisters and corridors of the college, stretching back to the 1880s. Martin's and my 'classpiece' is there, along with the others ordained that year, nearly fifty.

In the apse of the chapel are paintings of the six principal patrons of Ireland. As one of the themes in the decoration of the College Chapel is the preparation and training of men for the priesthood, it is interesting to contemplate these six paintings in the light of that theme. From left to right, they are St Laurence O'Toole protecting the people of Dublin from the Normans, St Brigid and her companions receiving the veil, St Malachy greeting St Bernard of Clairvaux, St Patrick preaching to the High King, St Columbanus building his church and monastery at Bobbio and St Colmcille/Columba and his companions heading into exile at Iona. While there is no evidence to suggest that the artist had any particular motivation regarding training for priesthood in relation to these six canvases, I have always been conscious of the themes that might be extracted from the images. Regarding religious

Figure 1: The Aisle in the College Chapel, St Patrick's College, Maynooth.

art, Robin Jensen offers four categories for religious art: decorative; devotional; didactic; and prophetic (Jensen, 2004, 100). It is in this final category that I think these paintings can be interpreted. What follows is a reflection on the six paintings and how what is symbolized in the depictions is still a very real part of the life of the priest.

Six Saints
In the first painting, Archbishop of Dublin, St Laurence O'Toole (1128–80) protects the people of Dublin from the Normans. The priest is meant to stand between his people and danger. Many graduates of Maynooth College since its beginning have done this, whether during the Troubles in Northern Ireland or in Apartheid South Africa. In 2017 the centennial of the Columban Fathers, originally known as the Maynooth Mission to China, was marked. Many of these missionaries did as Laurence O'Toole had done in Dublin centuries earlier. While there has been a strong tradition of standing between the people and danger, sometimes priests do not feel that anyone is standing between them and danger. Martin quotes Maloney on the six pressures facing contemporary Irish clergy (Maloney, 2013, 10–16): 'increased workload and consequent role ambiguity, loneliness and isolation, the fallout from the sex abuse scandals, difficulties prioritising and sustaining a prayer life in the midst of increased work, a lack of support structures (and perceived poor leadership) and the impact of secularization'.

One can see how the lack of support structures for priests might lead to a disillusionment in the mind and soul of priests. It can lead to a priest turning in towards his parish and ministry, and concentrating on what he can achieve there, rather than the problems and difficulties of the wider Church. Maloney also mentions the scandal of the abuse of minors by members of the Church: the very opposite of the image of St Laurence O'Toole.

Within the second painting, St Brigid kneels with her companions in prayer. It speaks of the need for prayer in the life of the priest. Maloney speaks of the difficulties of prioritising and sustaining a prayer life; priests busying themselves with the work of the Lord and neglecting the Lord of the work. Prayer is the oil which keeps the engine of ministry and life going and without it a priest seizes up and no longer functions spiritually. It is also worth noting that St Brigid is in prayer with her companions. With the exception of the occasions when he presides at the liturgical life of the parish community, the prayer life of a priest tends to be a solitary occupation. Perhaps this should not always be a solitary task. Priests would benefit from seeking out opportunities for communal prayer.

This communal reflection is also the subject of the next painting. Malachy greets his friend Bernard of Clairvaux. Now more than ever a priest needs the support of people around him. This is true of his lay friends and his family. These supports are essential, but the support of priestly fraternity is more important than ever. Maloney mentions loneliness and isolation, which would seem to indicate the need for a priest to stick close to his brothers in Jesus Christ. This is not meant as some sort of clerical bulwark against the ravages of the post-religious Ireland. It is a way for the priest to have the support of those who best understand his difficulties and his doubts. For a number of years, I lived in a presbytery with two other priests. We would regularly cook and invite other clergy in for lunch or supper. These were good and supportive occasions. What was sad was knowing of clergy who were never available to come along, with their excuses of meetings or rehearsals or too busy or too tired.

In the centre of the six paintings and somewhat hidden by the reredos of the high altar, is the painting of St Patrick preaching to the king. This reminds the student priest that the gospel is something that should be preached in season and out. Maloney speaks of the impact of secularization and this can have an enormous bearing on the spiritual well-being of a priest. To realize that some people are no longer passionate about that which you still are can be literally 'soul-destroying'. The Church of these first decades of the twenty-first century is marked by a declining church attendance and also something of a reluctance to take to heart the message preached in churches. It is one thing to love what we preach; it is another thing to hate what we preach. Worst of all is to be indifferent to what we preach. The cultural wars which have been waged in Ireland in the last few years and are still being waged have often seen the Church on the

Figure 2: St Patrick Preaching to the High King.

defeated side. While one can suggest many different sociological and political reasons for this, it still does not detract from the priest in the pulpit trying as best he can to preach the good news of Jesus Christ. Martin McAlinden quotes Michael Conway, 'significant changes at the level of culture are changing the very dynamics of faith and belief in society … this is having an enormous impact on ministry' (2014, 132). In his collection of essays on the subject of pastoral theology in 1963, Karl Rahner offers a description of a future Church:

> It is no longer a matter of family inheritance, but of conscious, personal choice; a considerable part of the riches of culture is no longer specifically Christian and may even exert a negative influence on a Christian's moral life; the Church will be a Church of the laity, where they will assume increasingly important roles and will take over many of the duties previously reserved to the clergy; the clergy will no longer belong to the upper privileged levels of society; the conflict will occur not so much between the Church and the State but in the conscience of the individual who is asked to make a choice between the values of the gospel and the dominant cultural mores. (Rahner, 1963, 23–26)

If anyone had told the Irish Church in 1963 that this was the Church of the future they would probably not have believed it. However as Littleton suggests, 'the reality in twenty-first-century Ireland is that although the Roman Catholic Church is still the majority church, at least nominally, it does not exercise the unquestioned power and significant influence it had during the previous few centuries' (Littleton, 2008, 14). Inglis suggests that the shift towards secularity has less to do with people becoming less religious and more to do with them, 'finding new ways of fulfilling their spiritual and moral interests' (Inglis, 2003, 43). He sees this change in Ireland as a process of 'de-institutionalisation' – the demise of the institution of the Church in various areas of public life, most notably the absence of religious Sisters and Brothers in Irish schools and hospitals.

> Being Catholic no longer permeates everyday life as it did a generation ago. To what extent are young Catholics being taught to say Catholic prayers and engage in Catholic rituals? To what extent has there been a decline in religious iconography, particularly the display of holy pictures and statues? In becoming less involved in the institutional Church, Irish Catholics have become more like their counterparts elsewhere in Europe. In so far as they see themselves as belonging to a religious heritage without embodying institutional beliefs and practices, they are becoming more like their Protestant counterparts. (Inglis 2007, 217–18)

This is the world in which the Irish priest ministers today, and for them it is less of an academic argument and more of the living the reality of the theories of Inglis, Taylor and the rest. While this might be the reality of the life and ministry of a priest today, he should never lose sight of what is important. The *Directory on the Ministry and Life of Priests* puts it succinctly.

> To rise to the challenge continuously presented him by the secularist mentality, the priest must make every effort to

protect the absolute primary of his spiritual life, his continuous presence with Christ and his generous pastoral charity, intensifying his communion with all and above all, with other priests. (Congregation for the Clergy, 1994, 37)

On the sanctuary wall, St Columbanus comes next and is depicted in the midst of a Celtic building site. The great sixth-century missionary to Europe is building his monastery and church at Bobbio, which reminds us that the priest is often one who builds. While one might automatically think of the building up of the Body of Christ, this picture reminds us that many of the nearly 11,000 ordinands in Maynooth's history have constructed churches in parishes and dioceses all over the world. Not only have they built churches but they have built schools and hospitals, convents and cathedrals. Some have carved out dioceses across the globe and have built seminaries and institutions of learning to sit alongside their alma mater. The reredos which I mentioned earlier is a legacy from Gerard Molloy, rector of the Catholic University and it was consecrated in February 1913 by the former president of the college, Daniel Mannix. He had been consecrated as coadjutor to the Archbishop of Melbourne in October of the previous year. The dedication of the altar was to be the last act that Mannix would undertake in the college before departing to Australia (Corish, 1995, 274, 296). His legacy as a builder in Melbourne can match St Columbanus and stands as a symbol of many other alumni of the college who did likewise.

The physical and spiritual building that is the ministry of the priest might result in what Maloney talks about in the increased workload and consequent role ambiguity. Many priests find that they are managers, builders, caretakers, fundraisers, etc., but rarely priests. They find that the sanctification dimension of their ministry seems to become less and less. In the midst of an increasing lay involvement in the parish community, their role can be diminished. They cannot do the First Friday calls because of an urgent meeting of the school board of management, so the lay Minister of the Eucharist deputizes.

Wonderful though this is, it deprives the priest of the beauty of the sacramental encounter with the sick and housebound parishioners.

Mention of Mannix's departure from the college in 1913 leads us to the final painting. St Columba or Colmcille is seen with his companions heading into exile at Iona in 563. Many of the priests who left to work abroad had no idea if they would ever return. The late Father Ronan Drury, former editor of the *Furrow* and Professor of Homiletics, would use the occasion of diaconate ordinations to relate a passage from Professor Neil Kevin's homage to the college, *I Remember Maynooth.*

> In this place of memories one is apt for many fancies. To see the oak stalls in the college chapel, darkening a little with the years, is to think of all who have been students there before my time and since. With no effort I can slip from the moorings of past and present, and see in this moment the years all rolled in one. The slowly moving line of priests down through the college chapel is never-ending; it goes into the four provinces of Ireland; it crosses the seas into neighbouring England and Scotland, and the greater seas into the Americas and Australia, and Africa and China; it covers the whole earth … it is unbroken, it is ever renewing itself at the high altar in Maynooth, and setting out again before the fathers and mothers of Ireland whose eyes are dim at the sight of it. (Kevin, 1945, 37–38)

Like their lay brothers and sisters, they could never have imagined a world where parents can keep in contact with children halfway across the world, and where grandparents can see and speak to their grandchildren over Skype or FaceTme.

What is evident in the picture is the companions who accompany Colmcille. Without the easy proximity of family in America, Africa or Australia, priests from Maynooth and other Irish seminaries banded together and supported one another. American clergy will still speak today to the FBIs (foreign-born Irish) as a term of endearment in some places and as a term of derision in others. They could often be a powerful lobby in dioceses and more importantly a powerful support for each other. A few years ago, I was locum in a parish in Marin county on the far side of the Golden Gate Bridge in California. I was invited to a clergy supper after the Saturday evening masses. There was just one other Irish-born priest apart from myself. There were also very few American-born priests. There were priests from China, South Korea, India and Vietnam. The days of the FBIs are over, but the importance of priestly fraternity still remains.

Conclusion

These six paintings in the chapel of the National Seminary give me pause for thought. *The Directory* suggests that the 'life and ministry of priests always develops within a particular historical context, as times replete with new problems and unforeseen changes, in which the pilgrim Church lives' (Congregation for the Clergy, 1994, 34). While things change, things also remain the same. Whereas the problems of a newly ordained priest from Maynooth from 1818 might be very different from those ordained in 2018, the fundamental principles which will guide him, strengthen him and hold him up remain unchanged in 200 years. 'In the current era of the life of the Church and society, priests are called to live their ministry with depth, anticipating the ever more profound numerous and sensitive demands not only of a pastoral nature, but also social and cultural, which they must face' (Congregation for the Clergy, 1994, 34).

To emulate the qualities of these paintings will make for a busy ministerial life, which brings us to the heart of Martin's writing on acedia. In the section on *Acedia and My Vocation*, he says that 'busyness of ministry had taken me away from my true self, from my core identity, from my reason for being a priest' (11). This is the danger of priesthood today. The overwhelming majority of priests are committed to their ministry and to the work of the vineyard, but perhaps less committed to their own well-being.

Throughout the years of seminary training, a prospective candidate for the priesthood has these six paintings as an object of study and contemplation. Every visit I make to the chapel conjures up images and memories of seminary years and priestly days. My mind is drawn back to the days when priestly ordinations took place in the College Chapel and I think of successive generations of ordinands looking up towards the paintings and contemplating the qualities of priesthood evident in the six saints. These were men filled with ideas and ideals and for whom the path of priesthood was varied. Martin has eloquently written of his path of priesthood and those to whom he has ministered over the years. His writings call to mind the opening words of *Gaudium et Spes*,

> The joys and the hopes, the griefs and the anxieties of the people of this age, especially those who are poor or in any way afflicted, these are the joys and hopes, the griefs and anxieties of the followers of Christ.

Sometimes the 'poor or in any way afflicted' can refer to those who minister rather than those who are ministered to. One of the lasting images of the six paintings is the presence of the community around the saint. Surely this is something that should never be underestimated or forgotten. I'll leave the final word to Martin, 'the whole of life is a process of formation and consequently the whole Church has a responsibility to ensure the well-being of its priests, as well as one another and the rest of creation. The role of the whole people of God in forming and sustaining priests has always been a part of the practice of the Church' (33).

Bibliography

Congregation for the Clergy. (1994). *Directory on the Ministry and Life of Priests.* Vatican City: Libreria Editrice Vaticana.

Conway, M. (2014). Ministry in Transition. *The Furrow*, 65(3), 131–49.

Corish, P. J. (1995). *Maynooth College 1795–1995.* Dublin, Ireland: Gill and Macmillan.

Inglis, T. (2003). Catholic Church, Religious Capital and Symbolic Domination. In M. Böss, & E. Maher (Eds.), *Engaging Modernity: Readings of Irish Politics, Culture and Literature at the Turn of the Century*, (43–70). Dublin, Ireland: Veritas.

Inglis, T. (2007). Catholic Identity in Contemporary Ireland: Belief and Belonging to Tradition. *Journal of Contemporary Religion*, 22(2), 205–20.

Jensen, R. (2004). *The Substance of Things Seen*. Cambridge, UK: William B. Eerdmans Publishing Company.

Kevin, N (1945). *I Remember Maynooth*. London, UK: Burns, Oates & Washbourne.

Littleton, J. (2008). Being a Catholic in Ireland Today. In J. Littleton & E. Maher (Eds.), *Contemporary Catholicism in Ireland – A Critical Appraisal* (12–24). Dublin, Ireland: Columba Press.

Maloney, G. (2013). A Look at a Priest's Life. *The Furrow*, 64(1), 10–16.

Rahner, K. (1963). 'The Present Situation of Christians'. In K. Rahner (Ed.), *The Christian Commitment; Essays in Pastoral Theology* (Trans. C. Hastings, 3–38). New York, NY: Sheed and Ward.

RESEARCHING ACEDIA: METHODOLOGICAL AND ETHICAL REFLECTIONS

Dawn Llewellyn

As a qualitative, feminist researcher one of the most exciting and stimulating aspects of working in gender and contemporary Christianity, particularly supervising students' undergraduate and postgraduate projects, is when I am given the opportunity to get my methodological 'geek on' and flex my research methods muscles to interrogate the approaches, tools, techniques, and ethics that are used in the disciplines and sub-disciplines of theology and religious studies. This tends to happen when an experience, in my fieldwork or in my students' proposals and empirical projects, seems to run counter to the prevailing academic literature, appear anomalous to the parameters in which I practice, or extends my current understanding of research methodologies and methods – something that all good research should do! And like all good research, by examining the contemporary Irish Catholic clergy and their experiences of spiritual burnout, theorized through acedia, Martin's doctoral work raises intriguing questions for conducting research. In this chapter, I focus on two ethical challenges prompted by the process of interviewing priests and Martin's use of his personal experience to explore the theological implications of spiritual malaise and disconnect: consent and accidental disclosure. First, I outline some of principles that underpin social research before exploring further the specific questions that Martin's work raises.

Qualitative Research in Theology and Religious Studies
Qualitative approaches are 'usually used when the object of study is some form of social process or meaning or experience which needs to be understood and explained in a rounded way' (Mason, 2002, 134). It is a way of accessing how people construe, experience, or produce their worlds using a range of flexible methods that are receptive to the

context in which the phenomena to be researched occurs. Qualitative methods interviews, focus groups, ethnography, autoethnography, visual methodologies and so on – elicit conclusions that are recognized as interpretive rather than 'objective' (Holland and Ramazanoglu, 1995) and can be adapted to give detailed and nuanced insights. Therefore, for Martin's work, a qualitative approach is highly suitable for researching the personal, fluid, and multi-layered experiences that comprise clergy lives and their accounts of spiritual malady.

Ethics are central to any research project that relies on the involvement of human (and non-human) participants and the onus is on the researcher to behave ethically – from the research design's inception, execution, analysis and dissemination. This might mean adhering to codes of conduct laid out by the professional bodies and academic organizations researchers belong to, or refusing to act in ways that violate ethical, academic or legal standards, such as deliberately misrepresenting data; using manipulative or coercive recruitment strategies; or exposing private information without permission. Part of undertaking qualitative research (or any research) is putting protocols and processes in place to avoid falling short of what is considered to be 'good' ethical practice (Bird and Scholes, 2011).

Qualitative research is a personal and interpersonal endeavour. Researchers enter into relationships when they embark on projects with the individuals, families, communities, or organizations and corporations they study. Usually, when I am introducing the enmeshed relationship between research and ethics to my students, I highlight that avoiding harm and maintaining participants' dignity and respect; communicating with participants and audiences; and making judgements responsibly are considered the cornerstone of ethical practice. In other words, research is a moral activity.

Towards Informed Consent

One of the ways that researchers try to uphold respect is through 'consent'. The British Sociological Association (BSA) Statement of Ethical Practice includes the following:

> As far as possible participation in sociological research should be based on the freely given informed consent of those studied. This implies a responsibility on the sociologist to explain in appropriate detail, and in terms meaningful to participants, what the research is about, who is undertaking and financing it, why it is being undertaken, and how it is to be disseminated and used. (BSA, 2017)

In addition to 'informed consent', the BSA states: 'Research participants should be made aware of their right to refuse participation whenever and for whatever reason they wish.'

Recognizing that participants have individual agency and choice, means, as Bird and Scholes suggest: 'we are obliged to fully … inform them [participants] with respect to our research and allow them the opportunity voluntarily to choose whether or not to participate' (2011, 87). To this end, Martin followed the usual orthodoxies: he applied for and was granted ethics approval through the Faculty of Humanities Ethics Committee at the University of Chester; produced letters inviting clergy and spiritual directors working with clergy to take part; advertised that he was looking for volunteers at clergy conferences; wrote a detailed Participant Information Sheet that outlined what the research entailed; explained his research questions and laid out his research design; completed a consent form that detailed the voluntary nature of the project; and emphasized participants' right to refuse questions and to withdraw at any time.

There are contexts where it is not always possible or appropriate to seek written consent: research on crowd behaviour; studying public events; in covert research when important matters of social significance are unlikely to be revealed through overt approaches; or with communities and groups who might find it difficult to work with written texts, or find it difficult to sign official documents (Bryman, 2004). However, historically, there are acute dangers for participants when consent is not obtained; the medical experiments conducted during the Nazi regime are often cited as the most terrifying example. Therefore the impetus and obligation to gain consent emerges from a need to protect participants, and it is based on the principle that participants should be made aware of what they 'are letting themselves in for' by taking part. Since Martin's death, one could argue that the grounds on which consent was initially negotiated no longer stands. His participants – his fellow clergy, his community – agreed to take part in the interviews based on the understanding that his analysis of their experiences would feature in his doctoral work and possible public dissemination; but this is no longer the case. In addition, the researcher is ultimately the custodian of the data. Therefore, perhaps, the experiences so carefully gathered in Martin's work and the knowledge it generates should exist – and perhaps should only exist – in the very specific context of the relationship of trust and the conversations that Martin had with his participants.

However, this response supposes that a researcher is omniscient, able to anticipate all the possible permutations and directions the research might take, and is in a position to lay out exactly what impact the research might have, or what might happen to participants or the researcher. As researchers, we can only attempt to be transparent about the research process, and what we need and want from the individuals, communities and organizations with which we work.

It also assumes that consent is a unique event that occurs only at the beginning of recruiting participants. As presented in much of the literature and in the University of Chester's guidelines and ethics processes, informed consent is assumed to be an unconditional, static, transactional agreement between the researcher and researched: participants sign forms and tick boxes; once they have read through the participants' blurb; and it is the researcher who carries the obligation to ensure consent is secured. However, informed consent is often more unstable than the absolutist way we treat it, and often requires re-negotiation throughout the research – not only at the beginning, but at any stage, and not necessarily with the participant directly. For example, with about one year to go to submitting my doctoral thesis (Llewellyn, 2015), I received a phone call. It was from the daughter of a participant, telling me that her mother (my participant) had died some months earlier. I had sent a copy of my participant's transcript through the post, but it had arrived after her death, only to be opened by her husband. Her daughter explained that her mother had never mentioned she had taken part in the interview, and what was proving difficult for the family – particularly her husband – was that in the interview my participant had expressed difficult and challenging reflections on her marriage, children, and her understanding of religion and spirituality that she had not shared with anyone. Her daughter, speaking to me on behalf of her father and her siblings, who would have found it too difficult to discuss this with me directly, was unsure how to move forward or even sure what if anything, needed resolving. This was because she understood her mother had consented willingly to take part and had freely engaged in the process – the interview transcript attested to this. In the end, I re-negotiated consent with the daughter. I first explained the terms in which her mother had agreed to participate, offered to send her a copy of the Participant Information Sheet and consent form, and I suggested that I would not use my participant's comments about her family or marriage. Like all aspects of research, consent is a moving target, it is not a fixed ideal, nor is it a neat process and rarely does it adhere completely to the researcher's plans and schemes, or the participants' expectations. In this instance, I was not even seeking consent from the original participant.

In Martin's work, it is not possible to re-negotiate consent. There was not the time nor the provision during Martin's illness for him to contact participants and discuss what might happen with their data. However, as I have suggested, informed consent is rarely enough as a strategy or principle – it is too precarious. But thinking again about the example from my fieldwork, I am struck by how my overriding anxiety was not consent, *per se*, but working with those concerned to protect the participant's and family's privacy. I am not jettisoning consent but it is often treated as an independent principle, and perhaps privacy is helpful when thinking about the status of Martin's data and where it leaves us when informed consent might not be enough.

Ensuring Privacy

One of the underlying principles of consent is discretion and confidentiality. As Spicker argues (2007) the main reason for obtaining consent is that,

> research is liable to be intrusive, and intrusion is only legitimate if consent is obtained. People have a sphere of action that is private, and theirs to control. Privacy is 'the claim of individuals, groups or institutions to determine for themselves when, how and to what extent information about them is communicated to others' (Westin, cited in Kimmel, 1988). (Spicker, 2007, p. 1)

Martin put several strategies in place to ensure that participants' privacy was kept intact in ways that follow quite standard procedure: biographical details in transcripts are anonymized and edited, but today we do not know how Martin did this, and in what ways, and what agreements he made with his informants. This process is usually approved by participants and often they are given the opportunity to read over transcripts to check they are a faithful record of the meeting and to be given the opportunity to change any identifying features. In addition, the original interview recordings have been destroyed (although the Data Protection Act states they can be kept for up to ten years) and Martin did not pass on participants' email or postal addresses or telephone numbers – we do not know how and in what capacity he contacted and communicated with participants. It would be almost impossible to establish who took part in the project. In some ways, if participants' well-being is primary in research ethics, for Martin's work, privacy might be a stronger and more robust ethical principle than consent.

While the discussion so far has focussed on permissions and safeguarding participants, if Martin's work is to be more widely disseminated so that we learn more about the meanings of acedia in the contemporary context, and the practical ways the Church can address it, then how do we continue to use Irish Catholic priests' stories, narratives and lived experiences, ethically?

Avoiding Accidental Disclosure

Usually in qualitative work, interview transcripts are used as evidence for the particular argument a scholar wants to make. Participants' words are quoted verbatim, a little like extracts from academic literature, and marshalled to make arguments, raise critical questions, and forward discussion. However, occasionally, when research is presented back to the community that is the main focus of the project, which often happens in practical theology doctorates when candidates are usually working with their organizations and institutions, there can be the potential for others to recognize a turn of phrase or an experience that is recounted. This happened to a participant in a research project on students' faith development at university. The participant was anonymized and most of the biographical details changed but yet, the interviewee has routinely been identified by readers of the text because of the way they spoke about the institution and the provision they happened to be criticizing. It has also happened to me. I took part in a project on gender and academic careers, and I did not exactly hold back about the inequalities inherent in the Higher Education sector. However, there are not that many women, aged between 35–45, who are Early Career Researchers but have the title of Senior Lecturer, in the humanities, who research gender and contemporary Christianity. There are even fewer who refer to themselves often and publicly, and in anonymized interviews as 'gobby' and 'outspoken'. I, too, was 'spotted' by various colleagues who recognized my views, opinions, experiences and idiomatic phrasing.

These two instances of accidental disclosure have caused little harm or discomfort to anyone involved. However, researching *acedia* is highly sensitive, and a potentially stigmatized, under-researched and unfamiliar research topic – Martin recalled in his work how he had never heard of the word 'acedia' until he was recovering on retreat. Therefore, there is likely to be a small pool of priests from which to recruit, in an intimate community like Irish Roman Catholic clergy, where networks overlap and are enmeshed, particularly when the project relies on word of mouth and participants share similar experiences and are sometimes already connected. In this example, what ways can interview data be used to further maximize privacy?

When Martin's principal supervisor, Wayne Morris, refers to Martin's data in the essay in this volume, he made it clear that participants had not given explicit consent to use extracts from the interviews: Wayne did not use direct quotations. It is possible that not quoting directly but paraphrasing or summarizing could be construed as misreporting participants' experiences, when researchers are accountable for representing narratives honestly to participants and to audiences. I often find this with students, the commitment to presenting work objectively in ways that coincide with 'reality' means they are very wedded to the exact wording.

As researchers, we want our research to be, as feminist ethnographer Kamala Visweswaran argues, 'believable' (1994). As a writer of theology and religious studies and lived practices, identities and beliefs, I work with people's stories, I listen to the narratives participants share, and I understand that it is already a representation and interpretation of their experience (McRobbie, 1982). Interviews are the product of a conversation, in which participants emphasize, minimize, leave out, edit, inscribe as they respond and react to the conversation prompted by the interviewer. This does not mean that qualitative data is 'not true' but the work we produce is always 'partial, incomplete, and detached from the realms to which it points' (Visweswaran, 1994, 1). One of the methods Martin was using – autoethnography – works on this premise. In autoethnography, the researchers are a source of reflection and knowledge-making. Carolyn Ellis, one of the pioneers of this technique, describes it as 'research, writing, story, and method that connect the autobiographical and personal to the cultural, social, and political … [its] forms feature concrete action, emotion, embodiment, self-consciousness, and introspection portrayed in dialogue, scenes, characterization, and plot. Thus autoethnography claims the conventions of literary writing' (Ellis, 2004, xix). Martin acknowledged that his personal experience was the impetus for his research, and that writing autoethnographically was a theological enterprise because it was a form of attentiveness and prayer that could 'pave the way for spiritual growth and transformation' (McAlinden, 2014, 13). It is also a way of critically interrogating his assumptions and experiences, alongside those of his participants. While we do not know the extent to which Martin would have adopted literary devices akin to fiction, his methodological choice is suggestive of other ways of presenting interviews than just including quotations. For instance, Christine Bold develops the notion of 'representative constructions' (2011, 145 ff.). In her research with second-year undergraduates, she used a survey to assess their use of reflective diaries. Rather than presenting the findings through themes, percentages, or codes, she used the data to create two fictional narratives, constructing an account of the diaries from the survey – one character called Una who found the diaries useful; another called Duet, who represented the students who thought the diaries were unhelpful. For Bold, representative constructions 'suggest the story is constructed to represent a particular type of person or set of events' (Bold, 2011, 145–46). Such techniques, which Martin was already exploring, could be a potentially effective way to privilege meaning, feelings, dialogue, emotions, the meanings of acedia, and honouring the experiences he gathered, rather than specific details attributed to specific participants (Ellis, 2004).

For me, Martin's astute, scholarly, creative and carefully held project highlights acutely that it is impossible to fully anticipate how the research process will unfold. Consent is fragile, and is not a one-off, never-to-be-repeated event, but should be extended throughout the stages of the research and be thought of as an ongoing negotiation – sometimes beyond the researcher's involvement. Therefore, as I have suggested, in such instances, perhaps privacy gives our ethical agreements with participants more weight. Research rarely goes to plan, but is, Mason (2002) points out, organic. It is also dynamic, messy, confusing, complex, (Kelly, Burton and Regan, 1994, 46) because we have to work with unforeseen events and encounters that mean we have to adapt or even abandon our initial plan – in part because we are working with people's anxieties and concerns, their lives and their deaths, and all we can hope to do is honour the fragments of the stories we are given to look after.

Bibliography

Bird, F., & Scholes, L. L. (2011). Research Ethics. In M. Stausberg, & S. Engler (Eds.), *The Routledge Handbook of Research Methods in the Study of Religion* (81–105). London, UK: Routledge.

Bold, C. (2011). *Using Narrative in Research*. London, UK: SAGE Publications.

British Sociological Association (2017). *Statement of Ethical Practice*. Durham, UK: BSA Publications.

Bryman, A. (2004). *Social Research Methods* (2nd ed.), Oxford, UK: Oxford University Press.

Ellis, C. (2004). *The Ethnographic I: A Methodological Novel about Autoethnography*, Walnut Creek, CA: AltaMira Press.

Holland, J., & Ramazanoglu, C. (1995). Accounting for Sexuality, Living Sexual Politics: Can Feminist Research be Valid? In J. Holland, M. Blair, & S. Sheldon (Eds.), *Debates and Issues in Feminist Research and Pedagogy* (273–91). Clevedon, UK: Multilingual Matters.

Kelly, L., Burton, S., & Regan, L. (1994). Researching Women's Lives or Researching Women's Oppression? Reflections on what Constitutes Feminist Research. In J. Purvis & M. Maynard (Eds.), *Researching Women's Lives from a Feminist Perspective* (27–48). London, UK: Taylor and Francis.

Llewellyn, D. (2015). *Reading, Feminism, and Spirituality: Troubling the Waves*. London: Palgrave.

Mason, J. (2002). *Qualitative Researching*. London, UK: SAGE Publications.

McAlinden, M. (2014). Living Baptismally: Nurturing a Spirituality for Priestly Wellbeing. *Practical Theology*, 7(4), 268–79.

McRobbie, A. (1982). The Politics of Feminist Research: Between Talk, Text and Action. *Feminist Review*, 12(1), 46–57.

Spicker, P. (2007). Research Without Consent. *Social Research Update*. Winter, 51, 1–4. Guildford, UK: University of Surrey. http://sru.soc.surrey.ac.uk/SRU51.pdf

Visweswaran, K. (1994). *Fictions of Feminist Ethnography*. Minneapolis, MN: University of Minnesota Press.

BURNED OUT, STRESSED OR JUST PLAIN TIRED

Ruth Craig

I first met Father Martin McAlinden in 2004 and as time went on we became firm friends. Martin and I had gone through similar issues in our ministry. He fully understood my struggle with burnout and my concern around actually 'surviving' ministry. We were both interested in the Professional Doctorate in Practical Theology at the University of Chester and in 2011 our Professional Doctorate journey began. At the core of our research was the desire to be and to do what God had called us to. We had both experienced crisis and disillusionment in our ministry. Martin found his answer in Worth Abbey and the discovery of acedia, my breakthrough came when I unwittingly stumbled into a supervisory relationship that accompanied a unit of Clinical Pastoral Education. Whilst our research went in different directions, the desired outcome was the same, to try to discover what actually happened to those struggling in ministry and identify skills and aids that could help prevent it.

Shakespeare wrote 'That which we call a rose by any other word would smell as sweet' (Shakespeare, 1982, 36). Similarly, whilst not wanting to detract from Martin's or indeed my own research, I believe there is something much more fundamentally important at stake. Whether we categorize this as acedia, burnout, stress, sickness or fatigue, we will see that clergy struggle. In response to Martin's work I want to examine the definitions of burnout, discuss some of the themes that have been addressed and finally offer possible suggestions towards clergy flourishing in their ministry.

Burnout
In 1974 Herbert Freudenberger wrote:

> The dictionary defines the verb 'burn-out' as 'to fail, wear out, or become exhausted by making excessive demands on energy,

strength or resources.' And that is exactly what happens when a staff member in an alternative institution burns out for whatever reason and becomes inoperative to all intents and purposes. (Freudenberger, 1974, 159–60)

In 1981 Maslach and Jackson produced the *Maslach Burnout Inventory (MBI)* (Maslach, 1986, 99–101) claiming that 'burnout syndrome' consisted of three distinct but interconnected characteristics which could happen to those working in the caring professions.

- Emotional exhaustion.
- Depersonalization.
- Personal accomplishment.

Maslach and Jackson's work categorized high mean scores of the first two elements and low mean scores on the third to determine the scale of the problem (Maslach, 1986, 99–101). This was developed by Rutledge and Francis who modified the MBI to provide a revised model created specifically for clergy (Rutledge and Francis, 2004). Implementing the revised model along with the Eysenck Personality Questionnaire resulted in data which demonstrated that there was a higher level of burnout among Catholic parochial clergy compared to Church of England parochial clergy (Francis, Louden and Rutledge, 2004, 13–14). A further development occurred in 2005 when the Francis Burnout Inventory examined poor work-related psychological health and professional burnout in relation to Bradburn's (Bradburn, 1969) model of balanced affect which involves high levels of negative affect without good levels of positive affect (Francis, Robbins and Wulff, 2013, 321).

Research was undertaken with ministers from the United Reformed Church in England (Charlton et al., 2009). This study used an open-ended questionnaire and concluded that ministers of word and sacrament within the United Reformed Church in England were exposed to recurring recognizable sources of stress. Whilst acknowledging that clergy obtained high levels of satisfaction from their ministry it also recognized that they were suffering from high levels of negative affect that should not be ignored or played down as a result of the 'job satisfaction' (Charlton, 2009, 148). The paper highlighted six key issues:

- Notion of balanced affect, highlighted the positive side of ministry.
- How clergy conceptualized stress.
- Differentiation between stress and burnout.
- Identification of triggers of stress within their own ministerial experience.
- Wider lifestyle issues.
- The wider Church role in promoting work-related psychological health of ministers of word and sacrament.

It identified three characteristics of stress:

- Pressure of too much to do.
- Feeling inadequate and out of control.
- Mismatch of expectations.

Along with five marks of burnout:

- Inability to function or carry on.
- Physical, emotional, spiritual shut down.
- Exhaustion.
- Response to continuous excessive pressure.
- Depression and clinical anxiety.

It then recommended three ways of keeping healthy:

- Healthy living.
- Time off/holidays.
- Prayer and reflection.

Concluding with five strategic areas:

- Ensuring ministers have their time off and holidays.
- Establishing reasonable expectations of ministers.
- Availability of formal support.

- Informal support from church members, family and friends.
- Bringing clergy stress to the attention of the church.

The report concludes:

> Here are a group of dedicated men and women who are aware of suffering from high levels of negative affect and who yet succeed in deriving high levels of satisfaction from their ministry. A responsible Church should not, however, allow the high level of positive affect acknowledged by the ministers to mask the effects of high levels of negative affect. (Charlton et al., 2009, 147–48).

Having examined some of the ways that research into burnout has been conducted, I now want to examine research undertaken in Ireland.

Clergy in Crisis in Ireland

Very little has been written regarding clergy crisis in Ireland, which makes Martin's research both relevant and important. In March 2006 a short article appeared in the *Irish Journal of Psychological Medicine* reporting that there had been no empirical studies to examine levels of burnout among clergy in Ireland (Lewis, Francis, Turton and Cruise, 2006, 40). The article claimed that burnout was linked with increased time off sick, clergy leaving ministry, or taking early retirement and even suicide.

Within my own tradition, the Methodist Conference in Ireland presented the 'Health of Ministers Report' in the same year (Methodist Church in Ireland, 2006). This was the outcome of a memorial to the 2004 Conference that a Working Group should be set up in order to examine the issue of the health of ministers. Part of that report consisted of the results of a questionnaire that was sent to 124 ministers in active ministry and 75 (60%) ministers returned the completed questionnaire. Included in this report were comments to do with having to endure high levels of personal abuse, dealing with difficult leaders, coping with bullying and manipulative members who behave that way in order to get what they want. There were also comments about unachievable demands of members – 'you can never do enough' and 'being expected to be all things to all people'; 'unfair/unreasonable expectations'. When asked if they thought stress had contributed to a health problem, 33% did not reply or stated 'don't know'. However, 84% of those who replied stated that it was likely or very likely. When clergy were asked to suggest at least one action which could be taken to support and equip ministers better, 48% suggested confidential pastoral care/counselling, 33% suggested more informal 'get togethers', training days and retreats. Recommendations included that ministers take two days off a week and form a small support group with people outside of the Circuit.

Whilst Martin and I are from different denominations we both experienced a difficult time within our ministry. I categorized it as 'burnout', Martin as 'acedia', however, there are certain similarities despite definitions. I want to address some of those similarities and examine preventative recommendations and suggestions.

Loneliness and Disillusionment

Some of the difficulties expressed in Martin's research are evidenced in the two reports shown above. Disillusionment, isolation and lack of group support seem to be issues that occur throughout denominations. There have been inevitable changes within ministry, particularly in rural churches in England with pastoral restructuring now leaving ministers with responsibility for four or more parishes leading to 'considerable local discontent' (Rees and Francis, 1991, 47). This is not only true of rural churches in England but in Ireland (Sheridan, 2015) and not just for the priesthood. Fewer ministers and changes in ministry are impacting clergy in all denominations. The 'apprenticeship' model that would have involved a senior minister being in close proximity with a less experienced minister is no longer viable and it would appear that it is 'primarily in multi-parish benefices that the clergy begin to experience premature ministry burnout' (Rees and Francis, 1991, 47).

Ministerial Training and Ongoing Development

Ministerial training and ongoing development could be improved upon to help clergy avoid difficulty. Martin was involved in ongoing pastoral supervision but yet in his own words it seemed that this in itself was not enough to prevent acedia in his own life. Whilst not true in Martin's case, supervision can often focus purely on the managerial function where a superior keeps an eye to the work we do and how we do it. However, this is only one of the functions, and for supervision to be supervision it needs to include the two other supportive and educational functions (Hawkins and Shohet, 2007, 57–58). It seems that Martin's experience is backed by evidence from a study which researched the hypothesis that clergy who had a positive attitude towards supervision and reflective ministry were less likely to suffer burnout. The results did not provide much evidence to support that theory, although it did reveal that clergy who expected to partake of supervision were likely to have a higher level of personal accomplishment than those who did not expect to have supervision (Francis and Turton, 2004, 262). Martin's research noted that often connections with God are discovered through experiential learning when traditional teaching is no longer helpful and recognizes the importance of both reflective and reflexive skills and good theological reflection for clergy (Thompson, 2008, 133). All of these disciplines, if taught well, are important tools that will enable clergy to navigate the changing face of ministry and begin to implement new patterns of ministry.

Prayer and Spiritual Disciplines
For Martin, his acedia was transformed through prayer and other spiritual practices and certainly the characteristics of post-acedia for priests has much to do with their spiritual life. Prayer can also help to counteract burnout. Turton and Francis examine the relationship between the attitude of prayer and professional burnout (Turton and Francis, 2007). Three main conclusions were reached, the first is the relevance of transcendence and the relation of that transcendence through prayer which positions all of life into a broader perspective of purpose and meaning. The second recognizes that if a priest no longer

practices the discipline of prayer then they may also lose confidence in the theology of prayer which could then lead to a separation from the vocational roots necessary to sustain and maintain their energy in ministry. They claim that 'prayer may well stand not only theologically but also psychologically at the very heart of Christian ministry' (Turton and Francis, 2007, 71). The third conclusion from this document was that both thought and action is required by church managers and bishops in regard to how they can develop, support and encourage clergy in their prayer life. It seems that a continuous and disciplined life of prayer is extremely important for the health of ministers. Doolittle also recognizes the importance of a minister's spiritual life and positive adaptive coping strategies (Doolittle, 2007).

Life Beyond Burnout

Fiona Howard explores the contribution that positive psychology has on well-being and how having a sense of coherence can prevent stress and ill health. Being fully engaged in work, feeling positive about the work being done and increased self-efficacy can lead to enhanced well-being and performance (Kalliath and Beck, 2001). Martin Seligman presents Huppert and So's definintion of flourishing writing that 'to flourish, an individual must have all the "core features" below and three of the six "additional features"'(Seligman, 2011, 27):

CORE FEATURES	ADDITIONAL FEATURES
Positive emotions	Self-esteem
Engagement, interest	Optimism
Meaning, purpose	Resilience
	Vitality
	Self-determination
	Positive relationships

Many people who continue to flourish in their job are people who recognize their work as a key aspect of their personal development identifying it as something that nourishes them for the rest of their lives (Hawkins and Shohet, 2007, 17). Some of the preventative measures that have been discussed above were also recommendations of a paper for reducing burnout and enhancing work related psychological health among clergy (Francis, Wulff and Robbins, 2008). Five specific support strategies were promoted by the church:

- The provision of sabbaticals.
- The availability of study leave.
- The use of a mentor.
- The use of a spiritual director.
- The membership of a minister peer group.

In 2013 further research was undertaken to identify if these five strategies were effective in reducing professional burnout or for improving work-related psychological health (Francis, Robbins and Wulff, 2013). None of these five options significantly lowered emotional exhaustion levels; however, two of them provided enhanced levels of satisfaction in ministry. These were:

- Having had study leave within the last five years.
- Clergy who currently had a mentor in ministry. (Francis, Robbins and Wulff, 2013, 328)

Further research into what that mentoring relationship looks like might be worth exploration. Does it incorporate good theological reflection, and keep an eye to the spiritual life and disciplines of the minister. Research has shown the importance of time being given to those spiritual disciplines along with a returning to the calling and vocation.

Conclusion
The church needs to be held accountable for supporting their clergy not only at times of crisis but in a way that is an ongoing discipline so that when difficulties arise they already have the skills and help available without having to seek them out. However, clergy also have a duty of

care to themselves. Ministers can experience isolation and loneliness and whilst recommendations can be made to encourage them to join peer groups or seek someone to talk to, it seems that this can require 'special effort, an exertion above and beyond the demands of daily ministerial life. And ... Actually reaching out to others may require a level of initiative and energy not available to them on a daily basis' (Scott and Lovell, 2014, 91). Is it purely that clergy do not have enough energy to engage with others regarding these issues or are there other reasons why clergy fail to openly acknowledge their difficulties? Is there a fear of becoming vulnerable and acknowledging perceived failure or weakness? And yet in doing so we are able to journey with others who have experienced failure and weakness. St Paul himself wrote 'when I am weak, then I am strong' (2 Corinthians. 12:10).

Clergy well-being and flourishing is not the responsibility of one particular group. As has already been stated, the Church has an important part to play, both ordained and lay, but clergy need to covet the relationship with God that initially brought them to the place of ministry. Carving out time and exploring innovative spiritual disciplines are necessary to help them to continue on in their vocational call and spiritual journey. Accountability is an important element and the best way may be an accompaniment of some sort, whether that be a mentor, spiritual director, supervisor or some other contracted relationship. Space is also important, space to think and space to help us live reflective, reflexive lives where our theology truly becomes practical theology that impacts our lives, our ministry and our pastoral care (Bass et al., 2016, 11).

Bibliography

Bass, D. C., Cahalan, K. A., Miller-McLemore, B. J., Nieman, J. R., & Scharen, C. B. (2016). *Christian Practical Wisdom: What it is, Why it Matters*. Grand Rapids, MI: William B. Eerdmans Publishing Company.

Bradburn, N. M. (1969). *The Structure of Psychological Well-Being*. Chicago, IL: Aldine.

Charlton, R., Rolph, J., Francis, L., Rolph, P., & Robbins, M. (2009). Clergy Work-Related Psychological Health: Listening to the Ministers of Word and Sacrament Within the United Reformed Church in England. *Pastoral Psychology, 58*(2), 133–49. doi:10.1007/s11089-008-0177-3

Doolittle, B. R. (2007). Burnout and Coping Among Parish-Based Clergy. *Mental Health, Religion & Culture, 10*(1), 31–38. doi:10.1080/13674670600857591

Francis, L. J., Louden, S. H., & Rutledge, C. J. F. (2004). Burnout Among Roman Catholic Parochial Clergy in England and Wales: Myth or Reality? *Review of Religious Research, 46*(1), 5–19.

Francis, L. J., Robbins, M., & Wulff, K. (2013). Assessing the Effectiveness of Support Strategies in Reducing Professional Burnout Among Clergy Serving in the Presbyterian Church (USA). *Practical Theology, 6*(3), 319–31.

Francis, L. J., & Turton, D. W. (2004). Reflective Ministry and Empirical Theology: Antidote to Clergy Stress? *Hermeneutics and Empirical Research in Practical Theology* (245–65). Leiden, Netherlands: Brill.

Francis, L. J., Wulff, K., & Robbins, M. (2008). The Relationship between Work-Related Psychological Health and Psychological Type Among Clergy Serving in the Presbyterian Church (USA). *Journal of Empirical Theology, 21*(2), 166–82.

Freudenberger, H. J. (1974). Staff Burn-Out. *Journal of Social Issues, 30*(1), 159–65.

Hawkins, P., & Shohet, R. (2007). *Supervision in the Helping Professions.* Maidenhead, UK: Open University Press.

Kalliath, T. J., & Beck, A. (2001). Is the Path to Burnout and Turnover Paved by a Lack of Supervisory Support? A Structural Equations Test. *New Zealand Journal of Psychology, 30*(2), 72–78.

Lewis, C. A., Francis, L. J., Turton, D. W., & Cruise, S. M. (2006). The Psychological Health of Clergy in Ireland – Who Cares for the Carers? *Irish Journal of Psychological Medicine, 23*(1), 42.

Maslach, C. J. S. E. (1986). The Measurement of Experienced Burnout. *Journal of Occupational Behaviour, 2*, 99–113.

Methodist Church in Ireland Minutes of Conference. (2006). *Health of Ministers Report.*

Rees, R. L. D., & Francis, L. J. (1991). Clergy Response Rates to Work-Related Questionnaires: A Relationship Between Age, Work Load and Burnout? *Social Behavior & Personality: An International Journal, 19*(1), 45–51.

Rutledge, C. J. F., & Francis, L. J. (2004). Burnout Among Male Anglican Parochial Clergy in England: Testing a Modified Form of the Maslach Burnout Inventory. *Research in the Social Scientific Study of Religion, 15,* 71–93.

Scott, G., & Lovell, R. (2014). The Rural Pastors Initiatiave: Addressing Isolation and Burnout in Rural Ministry. *Pastoral Psychology, 64,* 71–99.

Seligman, M. (2011). *Flourish: A New Understanding of Happiness and Well-being – and How to Achieve Them.* London, UK: Nicholas Brealey.

Shakespeare, W. (1982). *Romeo and Juliet.* Oxford, UK: Oxford University Press.

Sheridan, J.-P. (2015). Priesthood Today: Ministry in a Changing Church. *Irish Theological Quarterly, 80*(1), 83–86.

Thompson, J. (2008). *Theological Reflection.* London, UK: SCM Press.

Turton, D. W., & Francis, L. J. (2007). The Relationship Between Attitude Toward Prayer and Professional Burnout Among Anglican Parochial Clergy in England: Are Praying Clergy Healthier Clergy? *Mental Health, Religion & Culture, 10*(1), 61–74. doi:10.1080/13674670601012246

SEARCHING FOR COLLABORATIVE MINISTRY IN THE CHURCH IN WALES

Stephen Adams

Introduction

In many ways, my research journey on the Professional Doctorate programme at the University of Chester has mirrored that of Martin's; we have both wrestled with our respective churches' practices and sought to understand and humanize them. In doing so, I believe we have been striving to deepen faith and make it connect with 'fundamental human needs' (Volf and Bass, 2002, 18). Martin's friendship and companionship in this task have been significant for my own learning.

In July 2011, shortly after I first met Martin, I fulfilled an invitation from the Diocese of Swansea and Brecon to go to Rhayader and deliver a session about collaborative ministry to the clergy. I was no stranger to the diocese, having grown up near Swansea, been ordained in Brecon Cathedral in 1987, and served two curacies in contrasting areas. The session seemed to go well, given the constraints of time, and afterwards, I engaged in conversation with one of my former colleagues. He said how much he had enjoyed my session and then concluded with an innocent comment that did, however, cut me to the core. 'The trouble is,' he said, 'everyone is telling us that we must be more collaborative, but no-one is showing us how to do it.' Guilty as charged, I thought. As a parish priest, I had sat through sessions like the one I had delivered and wondered what I should do with the good advice.

Faith Without Action

Subsequently, I have discovered that rhetoric exhorting collaborative styles of ministry has been delivered with some regularity (within British Anglicanism) over the course of fifty years and more. For instance, the appeal in the 2012 report on the state of the Church in

Wales resonates strongly with themes identified forty-four years earlier.

> What is needed is a new, more collaborative, style of leadership, modelled by the Bishops and reflected at parish level. In the end this is about trust; letting people participate fully in decision making processes and then trusting them to own and implement those decisions. (Harries, Handy and Peattie, 2012, 4)

> The ideal in any parish, as we see it, is that the clergy and laity should see each other and work together as partners, rather than that church work should be regarded as the concern of the clergy, with the help of as many of their parishioners as are inclined to, or may be prevailed upon to give it. (Diocese of Llandaff, 1968, 35)

The reiteration of this appeal for collaborative working in report after report (e.g. Church in Wales, 2004, 2013; Church of England, 1985, 80ff., 1998a, 1998b; Harris and Startup, 1999, 199; The Faith and Order Advisory Group of the Church of England, 2007, 147; Tiller, 1983, 68ff.; Walker, 1973, 43ff.) suggests persuasively that there is a continuing and profound lack of achievement of these aspirations. The evidence from both my own experience, and that of those who participated in the research I am currently pursuing, confirms that there is a dissonance between the aspiration of the Church in Wales and the lived reality. The responses of Mervin and Doug, two experienced parish priests, are typical:

> the approach that I suppose I always find the Church in Wales has to teamwork and collaborative ministry is …, the best way to describe it would be tentative and at worst, suspicious. And, with an absolute reluctance to let go, to give too much. (Mervin)

> I think the church almost encourages you into a non-collaborative stance. I'm not quite sure what happens within the culture that encourages that, but we need to seriously look

at our culture and look at how we organise the church and to seriously ask questions of it ... there's a rigid pecking order in the diocese, and we all know that; the bishop, the archdeacons, the dean, you know; but does anybody ever question that pecking order, does anybody question the culture? (Doug)

All this indicates that what is required is something more fundamental than a convincing argument (theological or otherwise) for the necessity of collaborative ministry. Even the contention that the problem will be solved by training up a fresh generation of 'new style' collaborative clergy and laity looks thin in the light of the decades over which the aspiration has repeatedly been stated.

Ministry Moves

Stephen Pickard (2009, 1), labels this problem as an assumption that collaborative ministry will be second nature within the Christian community; however, in real life, he maintains, collaboration 'seems to require something of us that we lack the spiritual capacity and will to deliver'. He goes on to delineate seven moves that he believes are essential to the true character of the church and its witness to the Gospel (Pickard, 2010, 2012). The moves are interrelated and have the potential to shift the church from its present state of aspiration to being truly collaborative. The moves are:

- from Fragmentation to Integration.
- from Mechanistic to Organic Theory and Practice.
- from Competition to Cooperation.
- from Non-Relational to Relational Praxis.
- from Skills to Character.
- from Structure to Energy.
- from Servant to Friend.

Practice

What is implied here is that collaborative ministry is not so much a technique to be learned on a short course or a theory to which we give mental assent. Rather, it is a practice to be embodied and lived communally over time (MacIntyre, 2007, Chapter 15; Sennett, 2012, Chapters 7–9). In that sense, it is more a way of life that, in our present culture, is not necessarily an instinctive or natural mode of being (Brueggemann, 1999; Selby, 1997). As a Christian way of life, it expresses the life of the church and becomes something that 'Christian people do together over time to address fundamental human needs in response to and in the light of God's active presence for the life of the world in Jesus Christ' (Volf and Bass, 2002, 18). Practices do not in themselves constitute the church but are done in response to the initiative of God and are a means of faithful participation in the 'mysterious dynamic of fall and redemption, sin and grace' (27).

To dig deeper into the notion of practice, I want to focus on just one of Pickard's moves with a hint to a second; namely, the move from competition to cooperation and the move from servant to friend. I have chosen the first because of the problematic nature of power in relation to competition and cooperation; the second, because it presents the possibility of a relational ecclesiology that can transform the problem of power. Turning first to the question of power, competition, and co-operation, I will explore the reflexive sociology of Pierre Bourdieu (Bourdieu and Wacquant, 1992) as a means of unmasking its problematic elements.

Bourdieu and Practice
Bourdieu understands practice to be the result of the interaction of three interrelated components: habitus, capital and field and he offers the following formula to demonstrate that practice cannot be reduced to one element alone; all three operate in relation to one another.

> [(Habitus) (Capital)] + Field = Practice
> (Bourdieu, 1984, 101)

Habitus
Habitus concerns the dispositions, thoughts, feeling, and motivations that cause us to act or not to act in particular ways: to choose this course of action and not another. It is generated by the field or social space in

which we have grown up, been educated in, been most influenced by. Our habitus develops as we journey from our past to the present and evolves with us into our future. It is shaped by the social space or field in which we live and, furthermore, it contributes to and influences that same social space. (Bourdieu and Wacquant, 1992; Grenfell, 2014). Habitus provides us with a system of perception of practices and of their evaluation. So, for example, if we belong in a particular social space and know its rules and conventions we recognize when someone new is finding it hard to fit in. 'Habitus thus implies a "sense of one's place" but also a "sense of the place of others"' (Bourdieu, 1989, 19).

Capital

To understand the way in which social exchange is negotiated, Bourdieu advocates the retrieval of the term capital from the world of economics into other forms of exchange (Moore, 2014, 98). Thus, he proposes a broad distinction between economic and symbolic capital (which, itself, includes sub-types such as social, cultural, scientific, literary, narrative, etc.) (Moore, 2014, 100). The importance of this shift for Bourdieu is demonstrated by his claim that monetary exchange, in its focus on profit, has mostly confined self-interest within narrow financial senses while other forms of exchange, by implication, are portrayed as disinterested (Bourdieu, 2008, 280–81). Such misrecognition arises from the failure to acknowledge forms of exchange beyond the economic.

According to Bourdieu, misrecognition occurs when the exchange of symbolic forms of capital into power is hidden from sight because it is represented by other cultural values that are viewed, arbitrarily, as of higher worth and 'above' financial exchange. Just as in the economic world, capital in these symbolic senses is mobilized to increase capital, to control, to influence, and to effect action. Further, these other forms of capital have a value that can be exchanged for influence or control, etc. So, for example, groups and individuals with low economic capital but high cultural, social or symbolic capital can exercise influence above that determined at a purely economic level.

Bourdieu argues further that cultural, social and symbolic capital accrues to individuals and groups through the arbitrary valuing of certain conventions, norms and styles above others. Thus, in his research on the field of education, he highlights the way in which middle- and upper-class values are built into the educational system so that these values are reproduced in succeeding generations. Such reproduction ensures that controlling groups maintain control and continue to exercise power. That is, they continue to accrue cultural, symbolic, social and economic capital because their values are seen to be of the highest worth in the social field (Bourdieu and Passeron, 1990, Chapter 3).

Field

Field is the third component of Bourdieu's scheme and describes the social space in which individuals and groups operate and live. He refers to it as a competitive space, as in a sports field for example, where players vie for capital via the outworking of their habitus. Just as in sport, there are rules together with often unwritten regularities and conventions that a player must negotiate to develop 'a feel for the game' (Bourdieu, 1990, 64ff.). Through such negotiation, a player may attain a well-developed habitus within the field and, thereby, accrue more cultural capital. Due to the likenesses and overlaps between fields the strategies of a player with a good 'feel for the game' may operate as 'double plays', increasing cultural capital in more than one field at a time (Bourdieu, 1996, 271–72; Thomson, 2014, 70–71).

Importantly, Bourdieu emphasizes that contest characterizes a field: 'As a space of potential and active forces, the field is also a field of struggles aimed at preserving or transforming the configuration of these forces' (Bourdieu and Wacquant, 1992, 101). During times of social change when field conditions are altering many 'players' will experience field-habitus mismatch. Then the struggles (or competition) for preservation or transformation of the field will be at their most obvious. Moreover, an effect Bourdieu refers to as hysteresis (a lag) will come into operation as players resist the field changes, adapt their habitus, or withdraw from the field altogether (Bourdieu, 1984, 142–43; Hardy, 2014, 126–45). We can reflect here on the cycles of structural change that have happened in recent decades in fields such as education and health and that are now happening within the Church in Wales in its push to develop ministry areas.

Relating it All to Experience Within the Church in Wales

Bourdieu sees his model not so much as a theory but as a set of 'thinking tools' (Wacquant, 1989, 50). I contend that, as thinking tools, they can help us to understand the dissonance experienced by parish clergy as the result of a profound habitus-field mismatch that produces feelings of having become a 'fish out of water' (Maton, 2014, 56). The old patterns of being a parish priest shift from a pastoral ministry of word and sacrament within a single parish and community to managing a large group of churches and ministers (lay and ordained); the titles shift from being Rector or Vicar to Ministry Area Leader. All this leads to a sense that the rules of the game have altered and that 'I' no longer fit in. What follows is often a pattern of sitting it out until retirement, grim bafflement at the changes, or deep cynicism about the institution. For those who manage to adapt to the new rules, re-framing of the construct of priesthood and ministry is often necessary and painful (Fransella and Dalton, 1990; Hull, 1985, 32–34, 102–45).

Moreover, attempts by a diocesan hierarchy to promote the new habitus of ministry areas with the aim of re-forming the existing field can be perceived as 'a complete branding exercise' (Doug) that generates negative emotions: as Doug reported, 'I'm not sure what's behind [the branding] … and it just turns me off completely. I long for it to be a bit more real and to be a bit more grounded and to actually realise that this is going to be a tough battle [to change]' (Doug).

Likewise, appeals to the New Testament often function as a form of what Bourdieu refers to as 'symbolic violence' (Schubert, 2014) because of the simplistic way in which the text is interpreted. The frequent appeal to Paul's body of Christ metaphor concerning relations in the church (e.g. 1 Corinthians 12) sends a powerful message that competition and struggle are out of place and unchristian. The resulting culture of 'niceness' that is expected of both the ordained and lay stifles deep communication and appreciation of diversity and difference (Lederach, 1999; Savage, 2006).

Such a culture of niceness and its attendant distaste for conflict creates a space where the powerful can mask their symbolic capital (sometimes even to themselves) and become 'successful' in the church's field of struggles.

There are good examples of those who see in the gospels (and especially Matthew 18) a church working through issues of conflict, forgiveness and church order (e.g. Dunn, 1999). Whatever the original community situation that Matthew was addressing, it is clear that conflict and church discipline were high on the agenda from the beginning (Luz, 1995, 104–08). Similarly, in the Corinthian church, we see that the body of Christ imagery is clearly addressing a tense and conflicted community (Furnish, 1999, 30ff., 89–91). To appropriate New Testament verses and language as a simple descriptor of how things ought to be (e.g. Harries et al., 2012, 2–3) fails to recognize that language's own location within first-century social fields, habitus and capital. Conversely, to identify Paul's writing as an appeal to live out a different sort of economics (Selby, 1997, 154) is to employ symbolic capital originating out of divine gift, and to develop a habitus shaped by the Spirit. Such practices could allow the social field of the present-day church to be transformed and its practices to be grace-filled.

Conclusion – Toward a Relational Ecclesiology

I have explored the way that Bourdieu's 'thinking tools' and reflexive sociology have clarifying and explanatory value regarding The Church in Wales' ongoing difficulty in implementing collaborative team ministry. Nevertheless, Bourdieu's resolute commitment to social space as a field of struggles, and habitus as being marked by competition for scarce capital, presents a problem for Christian theology. If all social interaction is fundamentally competitive and characterized by self-interest, is there a place remaining for sacrificial love (e.g. John 15:13, Philippians 2:5)? Bourdieu, minimally, allows for such in the 'enchanted relations of friendship and love' within family life (Bourdieu and Wacquant, 1992, 98). In effect, the family is a special case that suspends market dynamics; but even there, for Bourdieu, emotional exchange is taking place (Grenfell, 2014, 165). Profit is everywhere.

In the study of collaborative ministry mentioned above, Stephen Pickard, tantalizingly, concludes his list of shifts in culture in the church with a move from servant to friend; but with little further exploration. Here he is evoking Jesus of the fourth Gospel: 'I do not call you servants any longer, because the servant does not know what the master is doing; but I have called you friends, because I have made known to you everything that I have heard from my Father' (John 15:5, New Revised Standard Version). Friendship, as a quintessential Christian practice and a vital mark of the Christian community (Braceland and Dutton, 2010; Moltmann, 1993), offers a way through the problem of self-interest and competition. Remembering Martin, I have confidence that Christian friendship, fully understood and embodied, might help to rescue the church from vain managerial attempts to revitalize its life and its appeal to the world.

Bibliography
Bourdieu, P. (1984). *Distinction: A Social Critique of the Judgement of Taste.* Cambridge, MA: Harvard University Press.
Bourdieu, P. (1989). Social Space and Symbolic Power. *Sociological Theory, 7*(1), 14–25. doi.org/10.2307/202060
Bourdieu, P. (1990). *In Other Words: Essays Towards a Reflexive Sociology.* Palo Alto, CA: Stanford University Press.
Bourdieu, P. (1996). *The State Nobility: Elite Schools in the Field of Power.* Cambridge, UK: Polity Press.
Bourdieu, P. (2008). The forms of Capital. In N. W. Biggart (Ed.), *Readings in Economic Sociology* (280–91). Malden, MA: Blackwell Publishers Ltd. doi.org/10.1002/9780470755679.ch15
Bourdieu, P., & Passeron, J.-C. (1990). *Reproduction in Education, Society and Culture.* Thousand Oaks, CA: SAGE Publications.

Bourdieu, P., & Wacquant, L. J. (1992). *An Invitation to Reflexive Sociology*. Chicago, IL: University of Chicago Press.

Braceland, L. C., & Dutton, M. L. (2010). *Aelred of Rievaulx – Spiritual Friendship* (Vol. 5). Collegeville, MN: Liturgical Press.

Brueggemann, W. (1999). The Liturgy of Abundance, the Myth of Scarcity. *Christian Century*, 116(10), 342–47. Retrieved from http://www.religion-online.org/showarticle.asp?title=533

Church in Wales. (2004). *Ministries in the Church in Wales – Working Group Progress Report to the Bishops*. Cardiff, UK.

Church in Wales. (2013). *Ministry in the Church in Wales: A Position Paper by the Bench of Bishops*. Cardiff, UK.

Church of England. (1985). *Team and Group Ministries: A Report by the Ministry Co-ordinating Group* (Vol. GS 660). London, UK: The General Synod of the Church of England.

Church of England. (1998a). *A Time for Sharing – Collaborative Ministry in Mission* (Vol. GS Misc 465). London, UK: Church House Publishing.

Church of England. (1998b). *Stranger in the Wings – a Report on Local Non-Stipendiary Ministry* (Vol. GS Misc 532). London, UK: Church House Publishing.

Diocese of Llandaff. (1968). *Report of Llandaff Diocesan Commission 1968*. Cardiff, UK: Church in Wales Publications.

Dunn, L. A. (1999). Transforming Identity in Conflict. In C. Schrock-Shenk & L. Ressler, (Eds.), *Making Peace With Conflict: Practical Skills for Conflict Transformation* (38–46). Harrisonburg, VA: Herald Press.

Fransella, F., & Dalton, P. (1990). *Personal Construct Counselling in Action*. London, UK: SAGE Publications.

Furnish, V. P. (1999). *The Theology of the First Letter to the Corinthians*. Cambridge, UK: Cambridge University Press.

Grenfell, M. J. (Ed.). (2014). *Pierre Bourdieu: Key Concepts* (2nd ed. Kindle for PC version). London, UK; New York, NY: Routledge. Retrieved from www.amazon.co.uk

Hardy, C. (2014). Hysteresis. In M. J. Grenfell (Ed.), *Pierre Bourdieu: Key Concepts* (2nd ed. Kindle for PC Version, 126–45). London, UK; New York, NY: Routledge. Retrieved from www.amazon.co.uk

Harries, R., Handy, C., & Peattie, P. (2012). *Church in Wales Review July 2012*. Cardiff, UK: Church in Wales Publications.

Harris, C., & Startup, R. (1999). *The Church in Wales: The Sociology of a Traditional Institution*. Cardiff, UK: University of Wales Press.

Hull, J. M. (1985). *What Prevents Christian Adults from Learning?* London, UK: SCM.

Lederach, J. P. (1999). *The Journey Toward Reconciliation*. Harrisonburg, VA: Herald Press.

Luz, U. (1995). *The Theology of the Gospel of Matthew*. Cambridge, UK: Cambridge University Press.

MacIntyre, A. (2007). *After Virtue* (3rd ed. Kindle for PC Version). London, UK: Bloomsbury Publishing. Retrieved from www.amazon.co.uk

Maton, K. (2014). Habitus. In M. J. Grenfell (Ed.), *Pierre Bourdieu: Key Concepts* (2nd ed. Kindle for PC Version, 48–64). London, UK; New York, NY: Routledge. Retrieved from www.amazon.co.uk

Moltmann, J. (1993). *The Church in the Power of the Spirit: A Contribution to Messianic Ecclesiology*. Minneapolis, MN: Fortress Press.

Moore, R. (2014). Capital. In M. J. Grenfell, (Ed.), *Pierre Bourdieu: Key Concepts* (2nd ed. Kindle for PC Version, 98–113). London, UK; New York, NY: Routledge. Retrieved from www.amazon.co.uk

Pickard, S. (2009). *Theological Foundations for Collaborative Ministry*. Farnham, UK; Burlington, VT: Ashgate Publishing Ltd.

Pickard, S. (2010). The Collaborative Character of Christian Ministry. *Expo. Times, 121*(9), 429–36. doi.org/10.1177/0014524610366079

Pickard, S. (2012). A Christian Future for the Church's Ministry: Some Critical Moves. *Ecclesiology, 8*(1), 33–53. doi.org/10.1163/174553112X619771

Savage, S. (2006). The Darker Side of Parish Life. *Church Times*, (7500), 13–14.

Schubert, J. D. (2014). Suffering/Symbolic Violence. In M. J. Grenfell (Ed.), *Pierre Bourdieu: Key Concepts* (2nd ed. Kindle for PC Version, 179–94). London, UK; New York, NY: Routledge. Retrieved from www. amazon.co.uk

Selby, P. (1997). *Grace and Mortgage: The Language of Faith and the Debt of the World*. London, UK: Darton, Longman and Todd.

Sennett, R. (2012). *Together: The Rituals, Pleasures and Politics of Cooperation* (Kindle for PC version). Allen Lane. Retrieved from www.amazon. co.uk

The Faith and Order Advisory Group of the Church of England. (2007). *The Mission and Ministry of the Whole Church: Biblical, Theological and Contemporary Perspectives* (Vol. GS Misc 854). London, UK: Church House Publishing.

Thomson, P. (2014). Field. In M. J. Grenfell (Ed.), *Pierre Bourdieu: Key Concepts* (2nd ed. Kindle for PC Version, 65–79). London, UK; New York, NY: Routledge. Retrieved from www.amazon.co.uk

Tiller, J. (1983). *A Strategy for the Church's Ministry*. London, UK: CIO Publishing for the Advisory Council for the Church's Ministry.

Volf, M., & Bass, D. C. (Eds.). (2002). *Practicing Theology: Beliefs and Practices in Christian Life*. Grand Rapids, MI: William B. Eerdmans Publishing Company.

Wacquant, L. J. (1989). Towards a Reflexive Sociology: A Workshop with Pierre Bourdieu. *Sociological Theory, 7*(1), 26–63. doi.org/10.2307/202061

Walker, D. (1973). *Swansea and Brecon 1923–1973. The Jubilee of the Diocese*. Brecon, UK: Diocese of Swansea and Brecon.

SPIRITUAL MALAISE WITHIN
THE ANGLICAN PRIESTHOOD:
THE CHALLENGES OF EQUAL MARRIAGE

Gill Henwood

Resonances

The invitation in Martin's research to live a reflective life in relationship with God is tempered by the revelation of the costly journey clergy may travel, with the possibility of encountering acedia along the way. Further, Martin's identification of the key themes of *imago dei* and *theosis* raise theological and existential questions about our identity and relationships as human beings, created and beloved of our Creator, relating with God and with one another.

Martin writes of an erosion of identity and a need for a discipline of becoming, with formation in the likeness of God through collaborative and collective participation in well-being. He asks, what is God like, revealed as Holy Trinity, and how can we strive towards God, calling our attention to the interdependence of the whole church. Martin argues for a commitment 'to stay in one's cell, to stay awake' (18) to be able to live a reflective life. His research uncovers the tension between 'allowing experience to shape a more mature spiritual identity and church' (18–19) and that 'suffering and pain and their destructive powers should never simply be tolerated and accepted but, wherever possible, should be challenged and transformed' (40). He emphasizes that 'developing resilience in the face of hurt and harm and seeking to transform the causes of such suffering are not mutually exclusive. Indeed both are crucial' (40). In particular, Martin raises the question of priesthood and celibacy in the Roman Catholic Church 'in the light of the destructive impact it has on its clergy' (40). Within the Church of England, priesthood with celibacy has become an issue for clergy who enter into civil partnerships.

My Research Context

I have officiated at marriages for twenty years, as a Church of England parish priest. My research question 'What is the meaning of equal marriage in the Church of England?' arose from conversations with brides and grooms who expressed a sense that they were equally loved by God and thus enabled to love one another in a reciprocal, balanced relationship expressed in Christian 'equal' marriage in church.

Other couples approached me, as parish priest, for a blessing of their marriage. Initially they asked for a ceremony after civil marriage, prior to 2002 when the Church of England permitted church marriage after one or both applicants had divorced.[4] Thereafter, requests for a blessing changed to significant wedding anniversaries with gatherings of extended families, or a blessing of new rings. Authorized ceremonies (Church of England, 2000) of marriage and of dedication, thanksgiving and blessing are public celebrations in a parish church with the parish priest officiating gathered with family, friends and occasional visitors. Couples receive affirmation, love and support; they feel accepted and blessed, not only by the parish community but by God.

By email, a resident couple requested a wedding or blessing in my parish church. They were both male. In conversation, I explained that civil partnership for same sex couples was legalized in 2005 but (before 2013–14) they could not yet marry under English law, civil or canon. To arrange a civil partnership they could contact the local register office or a licensed venue. But what could we offer as a celebration for them in church?

Pastorally, I sought to welcome the couple making a commitment to a lifelong, faithful and mutual relationship that clearly they intended to be 'marriage' even though English civil law only offered civil partnerships at that time. As practicing Church of England communicants, the couple had strong roots in worship and song, liturgy and service. The Church could not officially welcome

---

4 With certain exceptions, such as the new relationship being the cause of separation and divorce.

them – because there was no authorized liturgy – so we planned a Thanksgiving Eucharist, for the afternoon of their civil partnership. While two witnesses accompanied them to the register office, the couple's families and friends filled the church to celebrate when they arrived, sharing Holy Communion. Afterwards, both families expressed deep gratitude that the Church had welcomed them: they had been afraid their sons and brothers would be turned away. There was a strong sense and experience of the transcending presence of God with the couple and among the congregation: a sense of the sacramental presence of Christ and the hovering, creating presence of God's Spirit.

I experienced a growing concern and deepening spiritual malaise as I realized a gulf was widening between Christian living and the Church's traditional teaching and liturgy. I had served with clergy colleagues who were in unspoken, usually clandestine, same sex relationships in a context where no questions were asked. There was a private sphere and a public sphere, kept apart by custom and practice, with pressures on clergy in committed same sex relationships as well as on single clergy whose private lives were kept completely separate from their public roles, requiring considerable energy and compartmentalization.

From 2006, Anglican clergy were permitted by the Church of England to become civil partners, on condition that their relationship conformed to the Church's teaching.[5] In practice, anyone holding or seeking to hold a bishop's licence must affirm celibacy during the processes for selection, ordination and changes of appointment. Faithful lay communicant Anglicans became civil partners – musicians, organists, business people, teachers – who had been in their relationships for a long time and were often well-known and respected members of parish churches and local communities. However, the House of Bishops stated that Church of England clergy must not offer a blessing in public for civil partners and should instead pray with

---

5 'Sexual intercourse, as an expression of faithful intimacy, properly belongs within marriage exclusively' Church of England (2005, para. 4).

them privately. The Church of England made an uneasy compromise for celibate serving clergy, to allow economic and legal justice for same sex couples by permitting civil partnership.

In 2012 the United Kingdom's Government Equalities Office held a consultation on equal civil marriage, regardless of gender and sexuality. The Church of England's official response re-stated the traditional understanding of marriage as 'between one man and one woman'.[6] The government passed the Equal Marriage Act in 2013, with the first same sex marriages solemnized in March 2014. Civil partners could convert to civil spouses, with their partnership date on the marriage certificate. The Act's 'quadruple lock' protected the Church of England from legal challenges for discrimination, allowing church marriage to remain only for mixed sex (heterosexual) couples.

The reaction of the House of Bishops to equal civil marriage was to publish 'The Valentine's Day Declaration', as it became known,[7] on 15 February 2014 restating the official Church of England position: prohibiting clergy from blessing same sex partners and same sex spouses, and from holding a service in church for them. Same sex clergy are prohibited from civil marriage themselves, but may continue to become civil partners. Licensed clergy who marry someone of the same gender may not hold a licence in the future. While some same sex couples were planning their civil marriage with joy, same sex clergy couples in the Church of England thus received a clear warning (2014, para. 27).

Divergence and Exclusion

A mixed sex couple approaching a parish priest for a wedding or blessing can expect a warm welcome. Apart from divorce, where

6 'The Christian understanding and doctrine of marriage as a lifelong union between one man and one woman remains unchanged.' Reiterated in: Archbishops of Canterbury and York (2014).

7 The House of Bishops' meeting was on 13 February and official release date 15 February, but the significance of Valentine's Day (14) was noticed and widely commented on.

parish priests may refuse to officiate according to conscience, mixed sex couples can book a celebration, receive recognition of their marriage status and receive a blessing in public, surrounded by family and friends within their wider community. By contrast, a same sex couple seeking a blessing of their civil partnership or civil marriage discovers that the House of Bishops prohibits a priest from celebrating their relationship in a public service in church and from bestowing God's blessing, declining to authorize a Church of England liturgy. A priest, who in conscience would offer a blessing to a same sex couple coming in good faith to God through the Church, is required to refuse. The Government Equalities Office (2013, para. 4.22) pointed out that the Church of England's permission for the remarriage of divorced people in church includes a conscience clause, to protect clergy who decline to officiate. A conscience clause could have been an inclusive route for some clergy to *give* God's blessing for all civil partners and civil married couples, regardless of gender and sexuality.

Inclusive Church of England clergy – and their congregations – are deeply concerned to be required to discriminate on the bases of gender and sexuality by refusing ceremonies and blessing, thereby rejecting same sex couples in practice. For clergy who are civil partners residing in parsonage houses, sometimes with family members, there are additional issues. Partnered clergy who wish to marry will lose their vocation, profession, livelihood and future.[8] Martin's research revealed 'the stresses [celibacy] puts on clergy to conceal who they really are and to suppress this aspect of their humanity and the subsequent destructiveness this causes' (39). The Church of England risks, through the requirement of same sex clergy couples to be celibate, the possibility of stress for both people in the partnership, raising grave concerns about the suppression of 'this aspect of their humanity.'

---

8 The cases of Andrew Foreshew Cain, a parish priest who resigned to marry, and Canon Jeremy Pemberton, a senior NHS hospital chaplain who married in April 2014 and lost his appeal against the refusal to license him to a new post (Drake, 2016 and Woods, 2017).

When people seeking pastoral offices must be, in effect, turned away, a parish priest's personal sense of spiritual malaise deepens. Rather than to welcome in God's name, following in the way of Christ, Church of England clergy must act towards same sex couples in ways which result in feelings of exclusion, rejection and denial of recognition. Yet these couples are fully and legally recognized under civil law and within their community. The prohibition of clergy to welcome through liturgy and blessing affects families, friends, congregations, local communities and priests themselves. The prohibition creates dissonance, a sense of a lack of congruence with lived reality, when same sex couples are deeply involved in church communities and worship as clergy, organists and church council members. There is a direct, consequential impact on the Gospel message lived and proclaimed by the parish church community, because binary division based on gender and sexuality remains enshrined in canon law and practice. In practice, a parish priest is prohibited from expressing through public liturgy any sense that God is, or may be, present in the love found between the same sex couple.

By contrast, many affirm the loving partnerships of same sex clergy and loving marriages of same sex parishioners who are respected local people, and feel their own sense of confusion and malaise because they sense the integrity and congruence of the couples in relationship. Where, indeed, is God? Is the Church of England stating that God *cannot* be present in the love found by same sex people who partner or marry under civil law? Yet the House of Bishops has already recognized that two of the three traditional pillars of Church of England marriage are present in same sex unions: fidelity and mutuality.[9] The third pillar, the possibility of biological procreation, remains a major area of debate, given that many mixed sex couples are not able to fulfil

---

9 'The proposition that same sex relationships can embody crucial social virtues is not in dispute. Same sex relationships often embody genuine mutuality and fidelity …, two of the virtues which the Book of Common Prayer uses to commend marriage.' Archbishops of Canterbury and York (2014).

this ideal through age, infertility or disability, whilst others exercise their choice to prevent biological procreation through contraception, permitted by the Church of England.[10]

Same sex couples in civil partnerships or civil marriages living within the Church of England who follow Christian teaching and embody Christian values also embody a deep tension: that the Church does not recognize God within their love or union. Yet practicing Church of England Christians in same sex unions respond to God's call, exercise vocations to ministries including ordination and live affirmed by the Christian community and wider social world around them. Same sex clergy may have to choose: between their vocation, which requires them to be celibate, and their relationship, which may be a calling to marry. Clearly this has profound implications for the partner, who may not be ordained themselves but who is not permitted by the Church to become a spouse to their partner. Some clergy who remain in a civil partnership, whether affirming celibacy or keeping silent (depending on who asks and when) express a sense of being required to be second class: 'We are, but we're not.'

My research into equal marriage in the Church of England reveals a pressing need for new theologies of human identity to emerge, accompanied by new theologies of human relationship.

Theologies of Human Identity

What does it mean to be *imago dei*, in the image and likeness of God, male and female? As the diversity of human characteristics is being researched (Thatcher, 2015), theologians are questioning not only what it means to be human, but how being human in the image and likeness of God may reveal something new about the Divine.

How do we interpret same sex love in the light of the verse at the beginning of the Church of England's marriage liturgy, 'God is love, and those who live in love live in God and God lives in them' (1 John 4.15b)? Is the Church of England saying 'those who live in love'

---

10 Since 1930 and 1958, BBC (n.d.).

who are same sex do not 'live in God?' For if they do not 'live in God', where does it leave Church of England civil partners who are clergy and licensed lay ministers, as well as same sex civil spouses? Further, does this mean the Church of England is stating that God *cannot* live in them, or, that if God may be there (because God is beyond human limitation), the Church is refusing to recognize the presence of God?

Parish priests are prohibited from offering a liturgy of celebration in church and prohibited from administering God's blessing for same sex couples.

Theologies of Human Relationship

The liturgy of marriage enacts with symbolic ritual the union in embodied love between two human beings, both made in the image and likeness of God. Both are beloved, both receive new life through Christ, both receive God's Spirit and both are caught up into the life of the community of the Trinity. Both are incorporated into the Body of Christ in baptism, sharing Holy Communion. *Theosis* envisions that as God came among us in Jesus embracing our humanity, the risen Christ lifts us up into the life of the Holy Trinity, participating in divinity. Could it be that same sex couples within the Church of England are embodying love between human beings, made in the image and likeness of God, but at a new time in human society that reveals a widening theology of God, who is beyond gender and sexuality? Can the Church of England prayerfully seek openness to new insights inspired by God's Spirit that will change our understandings of human identity and human relationships and draw us into new understandings of Godself?

Conclusion

The deep sense of spiritual malaise of some within the Church of England priesthood acts as a spur to question, and to live and work actively for change. My research on the meaning of equal marriage within the Church of England will, among other points, show that some same sex clergy find the resilience to thrive and endure, living with great courage in vicarages, with their families, embodying 'the new normal'. Some clergy colleagues work for inclusion and change whilst challenged deeply by pastoral gaps they are prohibited from bridging. Others find it too damaging to remain within a Church context where there is a widening gap of incongruence between their deeply held faith in God's loving care, and the Church's laws and practices. Meanwhile, a few same sex clergy have chosen to marry and have relinquished their licences, testing the Church's prohibitions and losing their ministries. Martin warns, 'As long as the Church remains committed to its current practices on celibacy, priests in that Church must find ways of protecting their well-being and sustaining their humanity' (40). We have an urgent need to discern adequate theologies of human identity and human relationships that reflect our *imago dei* and God's saving *theosis*, bearing witness to God the Holy Trinity's loving purposes.

Bibliography

Archbishops of Canterbury and York. (2014, 15 February). *Pastoral Letter from the Archbishops of Canterbury and York addressed to the clergy and people of the Church of England*. Retrieved from: https://www.churchofengland.org/more/media-centre/news/house-bishops-pastoral-guidance-same-sex-marriage

BBC. (n.d.). Religions, Contraception. Retrieved from http://www.bbc.co.uk/religion/religions/christianity/christianethics/contraception_1.shtml#h4

Church of England. (2000). *Common Worship: Pastoral Services* (103–93). London, UK: Church House Publishing.

Church of England. (2005, 25 July). *Civil Partnerships – A Pastoral Statement from the House of Bishops of the Church of England*. Retrieved from https://www.churchofengland.org/sites/default/files/2017-11/House%20of%20Bishops%20Statement%20on%20Civil%20Partnerships%202005.pdf

Drake, G. (2016, 9 December). Canon Jeremy Pemberton Loses Same-Sex Marriage Tribunal Appeal. *Church Times*. Retrieved from https://www.churchtimes.co.uk/articles/2016/9-december/news/uk/canon-pemberton-loses-tribunal-appeal

Government Equalities Office. (March, 2012). *Equal civil marriage: a consultation*. Retrieved from https://assets.publishing.service.gov.uk/government/uploads/system/uploads/attachment_data/file/133258/consultation-document_1_.pdf

Government Equalities Office. (February, 2013). *Equal Marriage: The Government's Response*. Retrieved from https://assets.publishing.service.gov.uk/government/uploads/system/uploads/attachment_data/file/133262/consultation-response_1_.pdf

House of Bishops of the Church of England. (2014, 15 February). *Statement of Pastoral Guidance on Same Sex Marriage*. Retrieved from https://www.churchofengland.org/more/media-centre/news/house-bishops-pastoral-guidance-same-sex-marriage

Thatcher, A. (Ed.). (2015). *The Oxford Handbook of Theology, Sexuality and Gender*. Oxford, UK: Oxford University Press.

Woods, M. (2017, 30 April). The case of Andrew Foreshew Cain. *Christian Today*. Retrieved from https://www.christiantoday.com/article/first-cofe-vicar-to-marry-same-sex-partner-has-resigned/108149.htm

TOWARDS A VULNERABLE LOVE

Claire Dawson

Frost brings sharpness to the morning …
new light dances awakening
the early buds – crocus and hyacinth
the iris wanes
her first flowers shrivelling.
But around tight buds
remain
waiting
life moving
unseen
shoots tender, green, vulnerable.
It is time for an opening
to open again and again
to Her life
to allow Her rising
Her stirrings within.
The frost brings sharpness to the morning …

(Claire Dawson, February 2016)

I write poetry as a part of my spiritual journey. Expressing something of the unseen, the unfathomable. I used to share my poetry with Martin, particularly after he got sick. Sometimes I would email, or I would send a short text. I remember once writing a letter, that old form of communication that we have lost touch with but which expresses much more than the words it contains.

I am a priest, an ordained woman in the Church of England and without the unique opportunity of the DProf learning community I would never have met Martin, a Catholic male priest from Northern Ireland. Our worlds would simply not have crossed in the normal ecclesiastical bounds of our role. So I am immensely grateful to the

University of Chester and the opportunity it has given me to engage with such a rich group of people. As part of the DProf process we took time each year to share together our work and progress (and sometimes lack of it!) and so I have been journeying with Martin and his work now for some seven years. Since Martin's untimely death in June 2016, I have continued to reflect upon his work and discuss its implications with friends and colleagues.

What I offer now is a reflection on how I have interpreted Martin's work and see its relevance to my own context as a female priest in the Church of England. Whilst our contexts are seemingly 'worlds apart' the struggle for authenticity in ministry and a life that flourishes remains a mutual concern.

Martin introduced me to a paper written by Rowan Williams on living baptismally (2002). This seemed to be at the crux of Martin's work, the need for the priest to have their identity in and with the baptismal waters of Christ. Martin focussed much of his doctoral studies on gaining a deeper and more profound understanding of acedia, or spiritual malaise or sloth, the manifestation of what happens when the priest no longer looks after themselves spiritually. Following the work of Williams, Martin would suggest that there was a need for priests to allow themselves to enter into the 'paschal mystery' of baptism (McAlinden, 2014, 272). It was the priest's ability to hold the liminality of the chaotic waters of baptism that would help them to live more authentically. Martin talks a lot about liminality, the in-between space ... the chaotic waters of baptism into which we must enter again and again, the crucible and the chrysalis being the containers in which transformation of life may occur (McAlinden, 2014, 274). But this transformation of life only occurs if the conditions around are favourable and life enhancing. Taking the theme from the Desert Fathers, Martin often spoke about the 'heat of the midday sun' and the need to 'stay in your cell' (McAlinden, 2014, 273). It was the liminal moments within a priest's life, which, without a sustaining prayer life and a loving community would cause the deadly sin of acedia to take its toll.

Towards a Vulnerable Love

I am aware anecdotally and personally of the many ways in which acedia can have devastating effects upon the lives of clergy and also their immediate families. Leading to alcohol abuse, complete absence of any call or delight in ministry, marital breakdown, depression and workaholism. These and other areas are documented in Martin's work and I would propose are just as evident within the Church of England as they are within the Catholic Church in Ireland.

As with the Catholic Church in Ireland, the Church of England has also been managing general church decline and reducing clergy numbers. This has led to fewer clergy upon whom there are greater responsibilities. Instead of managing a single church most appointments are now for multiple churches. There is essentially more work to do and fewer ordained clergy to do it. Added to this, for the past decade the Church of England bishops have been following the mandate of a 'Church Growth Agenda'. This has led to increasing pressure being placed upon already stretched clergy to grow the numbers of church attendees on Sunday. The result has been, in the worst case, competitiveness between clergy and also sanctions or measures being enforced by a diocese on clergy who have failed to grow their churches. This is not an encouraging or enabling environment in which to work and certainly does not foster practices that would help the priest to flourish in his or her work.

The well-being of clergy is often spoken of as a high priority within diocesan structures yet this seems to be at odds with current models for ministry and leadership. Within the Church of England there has been a move towards adopting leadership and management styles from the business and finance sector. There are some positive learning opportunities here but there are also some fundamental concerns in the Church adopting models bereft of any 'theological or spiritual wisdom' (Percy cited in Handley, 2014). I wonder how these particular models of Church leadership may be interpreted through the hermeneutical lens of Martin's work: of the need for clergy to 'stay in one's cell and be resilient' (McAlinden, 2014, 277) and to allow the vulnerability of God to enter in?

It would seem that there is a sense of urgency within the Church of England to fix the numerical decline of clergy and congregations by becoming better and smarter at what it is doing. The issue that I have with this is that it puts the problem of decline on to the efforts of the clergy. If the clergy work hard enough and smarter enough then they will build a bigger church and help to reverse the issue of decline. What Martin was very careful to do in his work was to make sure the clergy did not feel the burden of extra responsibility for the failure of a system that they were unable to alter. Martin fostered the need for clergy to 'self-care' and develop habits of resilience but, he was very careful to stress that if the system in which the priest ministered was resistant to change then all efforts on behalf of the priest would likely lead to psychological and spiritual harm as opposed to flourishing: 'Resilience as a virtue thus demands courage to take responsibility for self-care, to challenge Church structures or assignments which are destructive and not life-giving, to know when "enough is enough"' (McAlinden, 2014, 276).

As a single woman clergy I have often experienced a profound sense of loneliness and isolation within ministry. The need for community and to be held within community was one of the areas Martin highlighted as a necessity in order to foster conditions which could enable priestly well-being and authentic living. He would often joke about the vision he had of himself when retired of living in the house on 'Craggy Island' inhabited by Father Ted. I think it frightened Martin to think about this sense of profound loneliness. In his work Martin touches on the too stringent a burden that the vow of celibacy places on to clerics. This is not a burden that I own myself but I often struggle with the profound effects of having to minister out of my own strength and resources. I have recently moved diocese from Liverpool to Sheffield. The experience of my move was a liminal time for me spiritually, psychologically and physically as I let go of one place where I had been known and lived and began to establish home and place elsewhere. Whilst I found the Diocese of Sheffield welcoming and supportive in many practical ways, the profound loneliness of moving and establishing myself as a single person in a new environment was at times overwhelming. I recognize that there are freedoms that I am afforded as a single person, which many who are married or partnered may find liberating, so I know that the grass is not always greener in this respect. What I am trying to draw attention to is the need for us as clergy to be able to be vulnerable and to hold our own vulnerabilities whatever these may be. These vulnerabilities need to be held within the loving and living faith community and therein lies a challenge for us all.

The 'Fix it!', 'We can do it better!' agenda seems not to want to know of this personal vulnerability which, if we are marked as disciples of Christ, we will all hold in our beings. Martin draws attention to the mark of the cross being the first symbol of baptismal liturgy (McAlinden, 2014, 272). What seems to be absent from clergy structures and current mandates is the permission and need for clergy to be held and to be vulnerable.

How can we therefore foster conditions that lead to flourishing and life? It would seem if we cannot foster these conditions within the life and ministerial practices of the clergy then I wonder where else life in all its flourishing should be found? As priests, I believe we are called to be 'other', we are called to be holy to hold people in prayer, we are called to discern the hidden whispers of God within our community, and to encourage the fragile new shoots of faith and hope to grow within the people of God. We are called to be silent when others are shouting for attention. We are called to be still when others are busy. We are simply called to model a way and to embody something of the divine within our own lives and beings.

Once acedia has taken hold it is a bit like bindweed and will take over and sap energy and life from the host. Martin was keen that good conditions of flourishing could be established both for laity and priests. He felt that to merely draw attention to the condition of acedia was like a diagnosis without a remedy. That an understanding of what nurtures us spiritually should be explored in drawing, music, poetry and creation as ways of developing patterns for resilience that lead to flourishing. We need to have courage to enable these work practices to be owned by the priest and for the priest to have the courage to confront the ecclesiastical systems, which has in my own experience often felt to be oppressive. As Martin would have said, we need to have the courage to 'stay in one's cell and be resilient' (McAlinden, 2014, 277).

I am now nine months into my new appointment in Sheffield. I do not know what the future holds for me within the Church of England. As I write this article we are ten days into the Feast of Christmas and on the verge of the Epiphany. I wonder as to what new revelation will be made for me and the Church this year as we wonder at the significance of Her incarnation. It is a liminal space, the baby has been born but we are yet to discover who She is. I wonder as to how the Church is going to make room for Her to dwell, I wonder how the Church's priests are going to be able to hold the paschal mystery? I long that my own vulnerability can somehow be held within the church community. In the holding there then is the possibility for the new and something else to be created from my own pains and the pains of those within the Church. I am often drawn to the work of Henri Nouwen and in particular to his book *The Wounded Healer* (1979). Nouwen talks about the need for ourselves to become vulnerable and that it is our own wounds that offer the hope and seedbed for the new. Or, as Mary Grey would say, 'that God is vulnerable, to be discovered in the soil of our vulnerability' (1997, 58).

The Paschal Mystery, which Martin refers to, is surely embodied within the resurrection, the dying of the old that new may come. The pain is that within the death, there is always the in-between space, the liminal space and that space is scary. The old has gone and the new has not yet come. It is in these times of vulnerability that we need to embody self-care and also to dare to make ourselves vulnerable to the Church community. It is only as we have the courage to begin to do this that new patterns of ministry may emerge which are more attuned to living authentically and baptismally.

Towards a Vulnerable Love

I have now been ordained for fourteen years and have about another twenty years of ordained ministry in some form or another ahead of me until I retire. Martin's life and death tells us that time is short and also that none of us know the time. I have experienced my fair share of pain, joylessness and depression within ministry. As I hold now this liminal space on my own ministerial journey I am determined that if my ministry embodies anything then it needs to be joyful. That I need to find ways of enabling joy to take hold within my own life; I need to make room for Her. Just as somehow miraculously room was made in a manger for Christ's birth so I somehow need to make room in my life for Her coming too. We think of 'the cell' being a barren place a foreboding place ... I think my cell needs to be bright yellow with sunflowers on the wall!

In this article I have reflected on what I have understood to be some of the main tenets of Martin's work and how his work relates to my own context as a female priest within the Church of England. I know that Martin hoped his work would be of benefit for male Catholic priests in Ireland. I hope that what this short piece of reflection has demonstrated is that Martin's work has a much broader application than the Catholic Church in Ireland. On my part I feel a renewed sense of conviction that Martin offered the Church a rare gift, an insight of wisdom. I hope that I can embody this gift well in my own ministerial practices. To be vulnerable and 'stay in my cell' and where necessary have the courage to challenge systems and structures which are destructive and not life giving so that there may be joyful flourishing and life in all Her fullness.

Martin did not want to die. He wanted his work to mean something to help release clergy into more fruitful ministries that may lead to flourishing and life. He knew of the wages against this both internally and externally and had lived the reality of his own walk with acedia. I hope he would be proud as to how we have tried to respond to his work. I hope he would be pleased with our efforts at wrestling with the 'demons of the midday sun' and seeking out a more kindly path. I hope that something of Martin's own life and work can be seen embodied in and through our work and lives as we have crossed each other on the Pilgrim Way.

Bibliography

Grey, M. (1997). *Prophecy and Mysticism*. Edinburgh, UK: T&T Clark.

Handley, P. (2014, 14 December). Plan to Groom 'Talent' for High Office in C of E. *The Church Times*. Retrieved from https://www.churchtimes.co.uk/articles/2014/12-december/news/uk/plan-to-groom-talent-for-high-office-in-c-of-e

McAlinden, M. (2014). Living Baptismally: Nurturing a Spirituality for Priestly Wellbeing. *Practical Theology*, 7(4), 268–79.

Nouwen, H. (1979). *The Wounded Healer*. London, UK: Darton, Longman & Todd.

Williams, R. (2002). *Living Baptismally*. Lecture given at Trinity College, The University of Melbourne, Australia, 14 May 2002, 4–12.

PRIESTS' INTEGRATED RELATIONSHIPS AND AN ECOSYSTEM OF POWER

Susie Collingridge

Introduction

The loneliness and isolation experienced by Catholic priests in Ireland today was identified by Martin McAlinden as a strong contributor to the spiritual condition of acedia. In years past, parish priests lived in community in the presbytery. These family-like groups (Friedman, 1985, 2) of celibate priests have, at their best, provided professional and spiritual support, companionship with peers and social interaction. In contrast, the contemporary experience for priests is of living and ministering alone in the parish or community. Martin makes a plea for improved sets of relationships with both lay people and fellow priests to ameliorate isolation and combat loneliness. This chapter will consider further Martin's proposal for the development of these relationships and propose ways in which they might be taken forward, avoiding some potential pitfalls. As an Anglican priest of nearly thirty years, with considerable parish experience while married and raising children, as well as some time without a partner, I bring an ecumenical perspective and personal insight as well as the slightly more distanced eye of an outsider to the immediate context of Martin's research group. My own research on Ministry Patterns of Clergy Married to Clergy illuminates the multi-layered dynamics of power for and around clergy, which I characterize in terms of an 'ecosystem of power' (cf. Percy, 2006), and I shall seek to explore how this model might also be applied to celibate Catholic priests in Ireland through Martin's research cohort.

Rooted Relationships – Families

Networks of relationships already exist in the families in which individual priests were born and grew up. These are often the settings where their vocation and Christian life has developed. They can be very positive places with the potential to provide important levels of support from those who know the priests as people beyond their professional roles. Not just parents, but siblings, their children, aunts and uncles as well as family friends and indeed former classmates, and childhood friends can provide perspective and support beyond the context of ministry in which an individual is known primarily in a role of spiritual leadership and authority. While those in the parish, even those of a similar age and outlook, might be reluctant to include the priest in spontaneous or planned social interaction because of his professional distance, his own family and other close friends have known him from an earlier time in his life and have shared history that they can enjoy together.

In their work on Clergy Married to Clergy in North America, Kieren and Munro (1989) identify social support as critically important for clergy. They define it as,

> a set of exchanges which provide the individual with material and physical assistance, social contact and emotional sharing, as well as the sense that one is the continuing object of concern by others. (Pilisuk and Parks, 1983, 138, quoted by Kieren and Munro, 1989)

For these couples, opportunities for deployment is constrained by the need to find an opening/openings suitable for both partners, which often takes them further away from their natural support networks than they would prefer or need, leading to a 'support gap'. Catholic clergy are more vulnerable, being entirely alone without a partner for mutual companionship.

Yet that family support itself is not necessarily without its own problems. These people, potentially well placed to support the priest through joys and sorrows may know him well, but they may not be within close reach. Many priests minister near their place of origin, but they can be asked to travel far from home to minister where they are needed, so individual clergy may be living a distance from the family in which they grew up, sometimes even many thousands of miles away and in an area foreign in culture and climate. While family and old friends might fervently wish to be able to offer support, and their continued love and concern is important in itself, it might be that their context and experience is so far removed from that of the priest, that it is difficult for them to empathize or understand all of the pressures that he faces.

Indeed, relationships with family may not be very positive ones in any event. There may be a history of tensions or even estrangement from the past. It can be that the process of leaving home to follow a vocation has been bound up with the dynamics of family life. For some priests there are complex relationships with his family of origin that are difficult to navigate (Friedman, 1985).

There is a need for an integrated relationship with family members, but, Friedman contends, it is important to be aware of triangulations and dependencies within the family system and learn to stand aside from them, developing their self-differentiation (1985, 296). This is particularly important for Clergy and religious for whom in some cases, following a vocation has enabled them to step out of negative dynamics of their family of origin, and they are intent on not being drawn back into a potentially harmful set of relationships. There are times when the dilemma is particularly acute.

> The significance of our extended family position … comes to the fore when we are called to serve 'professionally' within our own personal families, because we are never just another family member … we can get professionalized right out of the intimacy [of the family]. (1985, 296–97)

Friedman suggests that the answer to this dilemma is twofold: a) not being afraid to bring the expertise of one's profession to bear on the situation and b) to allow others in the family to be involved, and to be a 'coach' rather than a 'standard bearer' (1985, 297).

Healthy families are places of a person's first experience of love, care, emotional growth and acceptance and a network that includes people of different ages and life situations, provides mutual support and stimulation, but the answer to priests' need for intimacy is not a naïve return to their families of origin to gain greater support. Rather, it is through a maturing personal awareness that they are able to be part of that family network in a healthy way.

Close Relationships – Celibacy

Martin points to the doctrine and practice of celibacy for Catholic clergy in Ireland as being a major contributor to the isolation and loneliness that they experience and the development of acedia. From the very first chapters of Scripture, and the assertion that 'It is not good that man should be alone' (Genesis 2:18), through the development of Christian theology and doctrine, there is an understanding of the benefit of close human interaction and partnership for well-being. Nevertheless, the affirmation of the single life is present from earliest times in the Christian Church (e.g. 1 Corinthians 7:8), with celibacy now almost always insisted upon for Catholic priests. A change in the general insistence that clergy should be celibate may be beyond the influence of this chapter but it is certain that there needs to be a firm and active sense of responsibility for them by the Church leadership. The profound level of commitment by the priests to the single life must be met with an equally strong facilitation of opportunities for meaningful close interaction and partnership for them, not just as professional clergy, but as human beings.

The Celibate Priest and the Ecosystem of Power

The expectation of clergy deployability in appointments demonstrates the position of relative vulnerability in which priests are placed within the Church, exacerbated by systems of selection and of discipline. Priests may be 'acted upon' by the power of the bishop and the wider Church structures. Yet the priest is not at the bottom of the virtual 'food chain'; he also exerts authority and influence within a congregation.

In the idea of an ecosystem of power, every element of a social network has a relationship of power to every other. Power is not seen as positive or negative in itself (Sykes, 2006), and, therefore, does not lead automatically to actions of either benevolence or harm. Nevertheless, the greater the disparity of power between two elements, the greater the potential for either good or bad to result, indeed the vulnerability of the weaker party to harm is proportionate to the greater potential of the other to inflict harm by their action, or even inaction. Thus within a diocese, the bishop has a relationship of formal power over his clergy, while he is under the authority (and, therefore, power) of the Pope. Of course in a Christian context all of these relationships are notionally under the power of God, yet within the reality of Free Will, each individual has the possibility (and responsibility) to choose to act for the good of others rather than to harm.

I see power, then, as morally neutral, holding equal potential for good or evil and with force as varied as a fierce and relentless hurricane on one hand or a gentle zephyr on the other. Power is constructed and held within relationships and can be formalized by law and bureaucracy, whose rules themselves are sustained by people as they act and interact.

Within the wider concept of power some have attempted to understand different forms and elements of power, some of which can be seen as negative or positive in themselves. May (1972) and Litchfield (2006) envisage there being a spectrum of power; from exploitative, manipulative and competitive to nutrient and integrative – the latter two categories being definitively positive and the other three being negative (although it is of course contested whether competition should always be seen as bad).

In Torry's (2005) study of religions and religious-based organizations the author seeks to blend Max Weber's three types of authority (classical/legal, traditional and charismatic) with Etzioni's three types of compliance structure (coercive force, normative and utilitarian/remunerative), and concludes that 'an authority structure beyond institutional and social boundaries … [is] a major reason for congregations behaving as they do and clergy behaving as they do' (Torry, 2005, 176).

Thus in an ecosystem of power in church settings, there are potentially almost limitless nuances of power relationships. In addition to the formal elements there are also those based on subtle social interaction. While it might appear that priests have more power than congregation members because of being office-holders in the organization, ultimately members of the congregation can choose to leave the congregation if they wish, which is why some choose to exert power with threatening to resign from a role in church when they want something changed.

Where there are married clergy, one facet of their ecosystem of power is their spouse and any children they have. Resistant power could come into play, for example, if the spouse of a priest refuses to move parish because of their job or the needs of children's education. More positively for well-being, the power of family expectations can ensure that time is given to family relationships in shared meals and encouraging the priest to take proper time off, providing a counterbalance or buffering for the priest from expectations of the congregation. Single priests miss this layer of support but also the pressure from these close family relationships.

It could be said that the ministry of priests living alone benefits from having more time and energy to serve their parishioners, but it also means that any setting of boundaries or expectations has to come from the priest himself, which can be a cause of greater stress. Kieren and Munro (1988) studying Clergy Married to Clergy found that parish clergy struggled with theirs being a particularly absorptive occupation and they experienced a high level of boundary enmeshment, in which the areas of home and work life were hard to unravel. It is no wonder that Friedman (1985) emphasized the importance for clergy of working on their self-definition, to grow in awareness of their own needs and boundaries.

Historically, alongside their engagement with God in their spiritual growth and discipleship, the primary solution to loneliness for celibate priests has been their contact with other clergy.

Priests' Integrated Relationships and an Ecosystem of Power

Relationships With Other Clergy
In the past generation or two, living and working practices of priests in the Irish Catholic Church have changed markedly. Martin notes that a number of the participants of his study have seen such change in the course of their own ministries:

> twenty or thirty years ago, the general expectation and experience was that they would spend their ministries working in a parish with a team of other priests. More recently, however, with a significant decrease in numbers of those entering seminaries over the past two decades, the likelihood that a priest is now working as part of a larger team is much reduced. (35)

The effect of this change is very great. Where there were a number of priests working together in a parish, they would not just be colleagues, they would also be living in community in the presbytery. Friedman characterizes this arrangement as often functioning 'exactly like a nuclear family' (Friedman, 1985, 2).

Martin's implication is that acedic symptoms were less common in those days. While such changes may have accelerated in recent years, even at the time of Vatican II in the mid 1960s, they were already evident and warning signs of acedia were present:

> 22. Having before our eyes the joys of the priestly life, this holy synod cannot at the same time overlook the difficulties which priests experience in the circumstances of contemporary life. For we know how much economic and social conditions are transformed, and even more how much the customs of men are changed, how much the scale of values is changed in the estimation of men. As a result, the ministers of the Church and sometimes the faithful themselves feel like strangers in this world, anxiously looking for the ways and words with which to communicate with it. For there are new obstacles which have arisen to the faith: the seeming unproductivity of work done, and also the bitter loneliness which men experience can lead them to the danger of becoming spiritually depressed.

Presbyterorum Ordinis, Decree on the Ministry and Life of Priests
Proclaimed by His Holiness Pope Paul VI, December 7, 1965.

Within the context of huge cultural and social change, then, the effect
of celibacy on the priesthood is particularly dramatic. It is clear that
action needs to be taken urgently to address the problems for clergy
that have emerged in this still-developing situation. They will work
alone and return home to eat alone. They will pray alone and sleep
in an otherwise empty house. Not only that, but with fewer priests
being ordained, today's priests are both isolated as lone clergy in the
presbytery, and also managing an increased workload. If the model
of groups of clergy living together in the presbytery was a more
successful model than lone-working priests, how might it be possible
to replace, replicate or reimagine some of the support, collaboration
and fellowship of those arrangements?

Taking an idea from both multi-parish benefices and the minster
model of church, where Anglican churches in some areas are joining
together (for example, where there is a larger town surrounded by
smaller communities, or in larger towns/cities), could it be that clergy
from a number of parishes could be housed in a single presbytery, to
live together and travel out to their own places of work? Although not
all would be resident in their own parishes, the benefits of sustainable
ministry through community living, economies of scale and mutual
professional support could outweigh the disadvantages.

Strong expectations and practices derived from centuries
of theology and social development are hard to counter without
revolutionary structural and cultural change. One such is the
relationship between clergy and laity. Theologically and liturgically
the developments following Vatican II seemed to herald a sea-change
whereby the priest presiding at the Eucharist was brought into the body
of the church building, and the reflection on St Paul's imagery of the
Body of Christ (1 Corinthians 12, cf. *Presbyterorum Ordinis*, paragraph
18), may lead to further growth towards closer working between the
clergy and laity.

Relationships with Wider Community/Parish, Including Lay Leaders
Even where family relationships are weak or distant, there is potential
for priests to become part of networks of support where they minister,
especially if they remain for an extended period of time.

It may be the reduction in ordained ministers that proffers the
opportunity to develop lay ministry, but such a development is by no
means a new one, as St Paul makes clear (1 Corinthians 12). Even if it
has arisen for ostensibly earthly and economic reasons, the renewal
of commitment to the ministry of every member of the Church may
well be overdue. Collaborative ministry is considered in more depth
elsewhere in this collection by Stephen Adams (85–96), but suffice
to say, building teams of lay people and clergy has the potential not
only to revitalize the ministry of the local church, but may also help to
provide greater social support for isolated clergy.

This is necessarily a simple proposition, however. The notion
of clergy living in a goldfish bowl is common, describing their public
position and visible presence in the parish. As Peyton and Gatrell
(2013) write in their study on Anglican clergy, 'The public presence of
the vicarage and church buildings, especially when adjacent, signals
clergy availability' (2013, 48). They go on to say:

> finding the right public/private boundary in ministry is
> particularly difficult for all clergy and no clergy in our sample
> had found a perfect solution. Clergy are sensitive to local church
> and public intrusions into their private spaces: some are more
> defended and consistent, others are tactical from day to day.
> (2013, 48)

In terms of the ecosystem of power, the priest may have elevated
status in the institution, yet lay people also have power over the
priest in terms of their expectations and of the public gaze which has
a strong impact on behaviour and the internalizing of external control
(Foucault, 1977). Interestingly clergy appear ambivalent about such
intrusion, often choosing not to enforce boundaries as strongly as
they might, or to live with more flexible boundaries 'in favour of their

interpretation of obedient presence, identity and availability' (Peyton and Gatrell, 2013, 81) in comparison with the more segregated private lives of many other people.

Some relationships of potential support are complexified by dynamics of power and authority at different layers of the local and national institution from the congregation, diocese, national and global Church. While clergy may look to parishioners for support, more often than not they will be doing so within an unequal relationship, which clearly holds risks for those lay people who may find themselves vulnerable. Therefore, exemplary practice regarding safeguarding will be all the more important.

Development is necessary, therefore, in our understanding and practice of the role and function of the clergy in our Churches, shifting towards a more integrated understanding of relationships between clergy and laity in ministry, mission and Church life.

A sense of wistful nostalgia might lead to a sense of hopelessness that the social, semi-communal presbytery-living of the past is lost to the Roman Catholic Church in Ireland, along with the supportive close relationships and companionship that were engendered. Yet, even in the absence of a change to the principle of celibacy (or at least until it is considered more fully), the combination of developing new models of clergy living and growing lay ministry teams could help in reimagining the solution to the isolation and loneliness of priests which leaves them so vulnerable to acedia.

Bibliography

Foucault, M. (1977). *Discipline and Punish*. Harmondsworth, UK: Penguin.

Friedman, E. H. (1985). *Generation to Generation: Family Process in Church and Synagogue*. New York, NY: Guilford Press.

Kieren, D. K., & Munro, B. (1988). Handling Greedy Clergy Roles. *Pastoral Psychology, 36*(4), 239–48.

Kieren, D. K., & Munro, B. (1989). The Support Gap for Dual Clergy Couples. *Pastoral Psychology, 37*(3), 165–71.

Litchfield, K. (2006). *Tend My Flock: Sustaining Good Pastoral Care*. Norwich, UK: Canterbury Press.

May, R. (1972). *Power and Innocence: A Search for the Sources of Violence*. New York, NY: W. W. Norton & Co.

Percy, M. (2006). *Clergy: The Origin of Species*. London, UK: Continuum.

Peyton, N., & Gatrell, C. (2013). *Managing Clergy Lives: Obedience, Sacrifice and Intimacy*. London, UK: Bloomsbury Publishing.

Presbyterorum Ordinis, Decree on the Ministry and Life of Priests Proclaimed by His Holiness Pope Paul VI, December 7, 1965: Retrieved from http://www.saint-mike.org/library/church_councils/vatican_ii/presbyterorum_ordinis.html

Sykes, S. (2006). *Power and Christian Theology*. London, UK: Continuum.

Torry, M. (2005). *Managing God's Business: Religious and Faith-Based Organizations and their Management*. Aldershot, UK: Ashgate Publishing.

HOMILY: DOES RELIGION MAKE YOU A HAPPIER PERSON?

Elaine Graham

This homily was delivered at the graduation ceremony for Revd Dr Martin McAlinden at Drumalis, Larne, on 16 June 2017. It has been slightly adapted for publication here. The homily was introduced by a Bible Reading from 2 Corinthians 6:1–12.

Does religion make you a happier person?

Well – in true academic style – no sooner do I pose that question than I must rush to qualify it: 'Of course, it all depends on what you mean by "happiness" … and "religion".'

Certainly, there is some research to suggest that those who identify as having a religious world-view or philosophy, or who attend and participate regularly in a community of faith, also report higher levels of well-being and satisfaction in their lives.

But I rush to qualify again – what this does not seem to mean is happiness is some kind of facile, rosy-tinted optimism in the face of all evidence, or a naïve denial of life's sufferings and hardships. Rather, it seems to mean something much more complex: an ability to look adversity square in the face; an acceptance of sadness and setbacks, but with a capacity to cultivate endurance and strength to continue on life's journey. For me, this is perhaps described best as a kind of resilience: an emotional and spiritual capacity to take what life deals out and yet to keep going in wisdom and in hope.

And of course this was the territory of much of Martin's research, as the rest of this volume indicates: of actually uncovering, and naming, many of the stresses and obstacles encountered by those in formal ministry, identifying their causes and assisting with more constructive modes of training, and spirituality, and self-care. Not pretending that a sense of vocation, or privileged status within a Christian community, would render one immune to life's hazards – anything but. And of course much of what drove Martin's quest to undertake his research, and see it come to fruition, was precisely a refusal to collude with the silence, the conspiracies, the one-dimensional theologies and psychologies that fail to take these pressures and troubles as significant.

In the reading from 2 Corinthians, we are advised, 'Do not receive (or accept) the grace of God in vain' (v. 1). What does that mean? In this context, for Paul writing to the church in Corinth, it seems to suggest a Christian community that is devoid of that kind of resilience: of lives that have become so burdened and overwhelmed as to become arid, and meaningless. These people no longer embody 'life in all its fullness' – which Christians believe is what God has granted to humanity through the life, death and resurrection of Christ. Whether it is burnout, or internal conflict, or corruption, or lack of love – for oneself and others – there are many ways in which the church might lose its way and become empty, hollowed out.

But what would it mean for a community of faith to be restored, to come to a place in which it could regain its vision, and be rejuvenated by the grace and unconditional love of God? For Paul, it is a matter of ensuring that the church's life and actions get back in touch with God's new creation – which first and foremost means assuming the servant ministry of Christ himself – one of compassion and charity and vulnerability. As an example, Paul and his associates commend themselves as ambassadors for the Gospel not by impressive speech or displays of power, but by demonstrations of endurance and resilience in the face of hardship. But this only serves to draw attention, and credit, back to the way in which this is seen as a sharing in the suffering of Christ himself, in whose resurrection such privations are vindicated and find their justification.

Though persecuted and slandered, Paul was still prepared to see his own vulnerability as both a sign and an instrument of God's reconciliation. In that, he believed he was simply continuing what God had begun in Christ. To be truly authentic and effective, such a work would be of necessity risky, wounding and hard – because only then would it genuinely be a sharing in the work of divine redemption and Christ-like sacrifice.

To bear convincing witness to God's reconciliation is to embrace such vulnerability and face such trials. That means the Church being willing to put itself in the way of Christ by going to the places, here and now, where the world itself is damaged and broken and hurting.

Of course, the foundation of that resilience is not exclusive to people of faith and it certainly does not present itself in a naïve belief in a sky-God who will wave a magic wand and make everything better or protect us from anything that might cause us harm. Nor does it teach that God is punitive or judgemental, visiting adversity upon us in order to teach us a lesson. The truth is, we know that whilst tragedy strikes in many places, it does often bring its own bitter-sweet gifts of nobility and courage – and these are lights that shine in the darkness.

And just as Martin's ministry and research stood as testimonies to his passion for a more authentic and honest humanity at the heart of his own priesthood and that of others, so too his life – including his final illness – spoke of *his* courage, and humour, and above all resilience. In his life, and his relationships, he was a shining light, a beacon of God's grace in his own life and that of many others. His ministry was certainly not 'in vain'.

I will end with a poem written by an unknown Celtic author which expresses that gift more eloquently than I can:

An Irish Blessing

I wish you not a path devoid of clouds.
Nor a life on a bed of roses.
Nor that you might never need regret,
Nor that you should never feel pain.
No, that is not my wish for you.
My wish for you is:
That you might be brave in times of trial,
When others lay crosses upon your shoulders.
When mountains must be climbed and

Homily: Does Religion Make You a Happier Person?

chasms are to be crossed;
When hope scarce can shine through.
That every gift God gave you might grow along with you
And let you give the gift of joy to all who care for you.
That you may always have a friend who is worth that name,
Whom you can trust, and who helps you in times of sadness,
Who will defy the storms of daily life at your side.
One more wish I have for you:
That in every hour of joy and pain
You may feel God close to you.
This is my wish for you and all who care for you.
This is my hope for you, now and forever.

From Robert J. Wicks, *Prayerfulness: Awakening to the Fullness of Life* (Ave Maria Press, 2009), 166–67 (used with permission).

May that willingness to acknowledge the burdens, as well as the privileges, of his profession, and his ability to inhabit and impart that generous, life-affirming grace, be Martin's enduring gift to us. Amen.